I0828489

PENCIL DRAWING

STILL LIFE

Book One

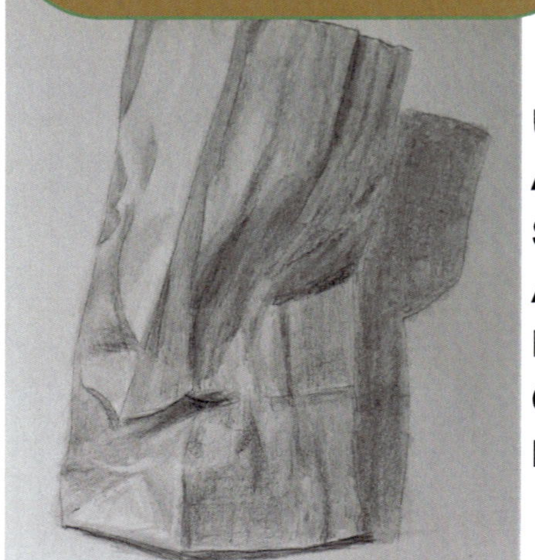

CHARCOAL DRAWING

Understanding and Applying Values

Shading Solid Objects

Applying Light to Landscapes

Creating Form with Human Faces and Body

PEN, BRUSH AND INK DRAWING

SKETCHING LANDSCAPE AND CITYSCAPE

Book Three

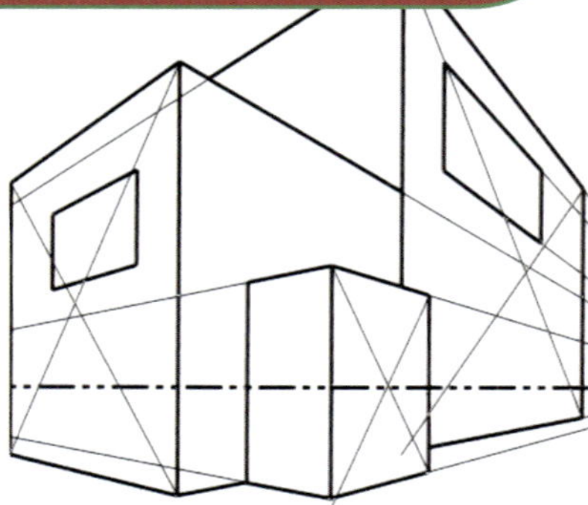

TWO POINT PERSPECTIVE

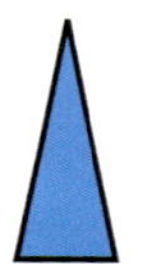

PENCIL DRAWING

Simple Geometric Shapes

Turning 2-D to 3-D

Drapery and Wrinkles

Patterns and Textures

Applying Still Life in Other Artworks

CHARCOAL DRAWING

FORM AND SHADING

Book Two

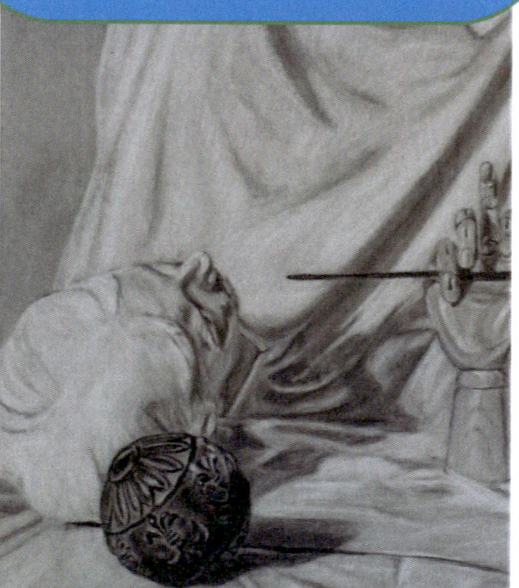

PEN, BRUSH AND INK DRAWING

Sketching Landscape, Cityscape and Seascape

Applying Perspective

Drawing Cartoons

Drawing with Ink and Wash

Working with Scratch Board

PASTELS DRAWING
PORTRAITS
Book Five

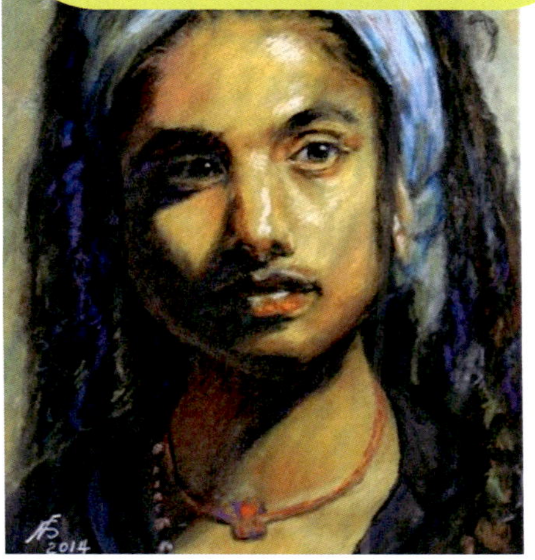

COLOR PENCILS DRAWING

Understanding Colors
Selecting and Working with Various Papers
Creating Textures of Various Animals and Nature

PRINCIPLES OF DESIGN

Understanding and Creating Exceptional Compositions
Creating Better Drawings

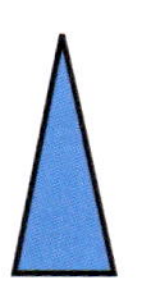

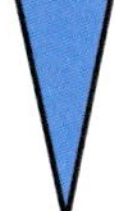

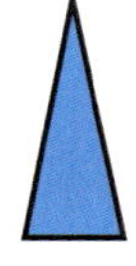

COLOR PENCILS DRAWING
NATURE/WILDLIFE
Book Four

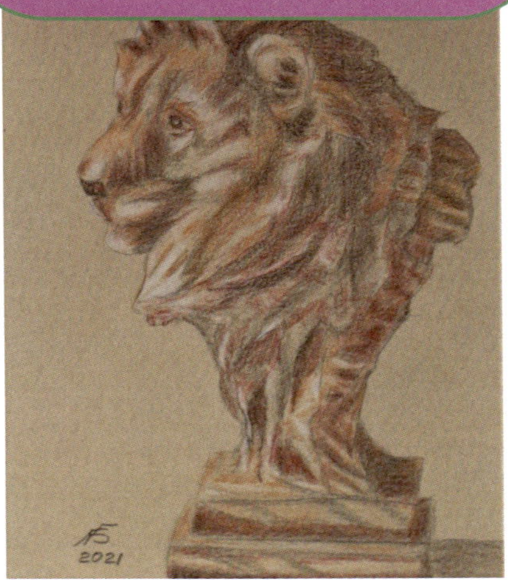

PASTELS DRAWING

Understanding the Emotion of Color
Working with Still Life
Working with Landscapes
Working with Animals and Portraitures

APPLYING THE PRINCIPLES AND ELEMENTS OF ART
Book Six

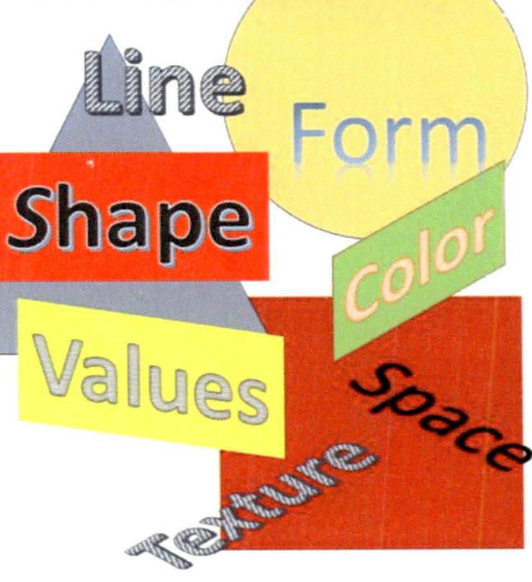

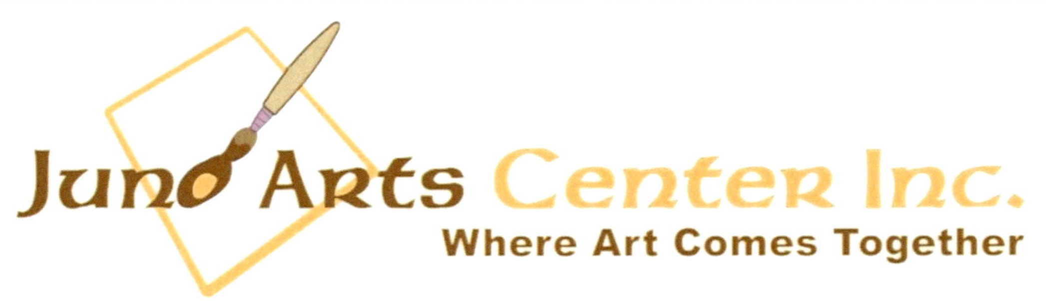

Norman F. Simms, MFA

Introduction to Drawing Series

Book Five

Pastels Drawings

Understanding the Emotion of Color

Working with Still Life

Working with Landscapes

Working with Animals and Portraitures

Acknowledgments

The author would like to acknowledge all the people who encouraged him to pursue his dream in becoming and working as an artist. He wants to give thanks to his parents, Leon E. Simms, Senior and Ethel S. Simms, for enrolling him in his first art school years ago when he was attending junior high school in Washington, D.C.

He wants to thank his wife, Dawn Chism Simms, for encouraging him to continue to seek a career in art and for continuing to push him to create beauty through his artworks. She is also the backbone of editing his writing. She is a blessing and a friend and they work well together as a team.

He wants to thank all the artist associations and art students who confronted him with many questions of how to approach and understand artworks and who encouraged him to write his books on various art related subjects. He also wants to thank all the artists and art lovers who are reading and viewing this book.

He would like to give thanks to all of the professional artists (Christine Hanlon, Warren Chang, Jennie Brunnick, Jung Han Kim, Sean Connor, and John Poon) who have given him a strong foundation for understanding the powers and the mysteries behind great artworks.

Norman F. Simms, MFA
Juno Arts Center Inc.
1-215-269-0390
normanfsimms@outlook.com
https://www.normanfinearts.com/

Autobiography

The artist, Norman Francis Simms, was born in Washington, DC in the year 1956. He graduated from his first art school, Art Instruction Schools, in 1975. He attended Murray State University on a track scholarship where he continued his education in fine arts. He changed his education path to study various Engineering topics at the Washington School for Drafting Technology and earned an Associate's Degree in Electrical Engineering Technology at its Center for Degree Studies. He later earned a Bachelor's Degree in Information Systems at the University of Maryland.

For many years, Norman worked for large engineering corporations creating engineering drawings and illustrations, but he felt he wanted to express himself beyond the commercial arena. His passion for his first love - art - became too strong to ignore. He finally attended the Academy of Art located in San Francisco, California earning a Master's Degree in Fine Arts.

Norman creates dynamic paintings and drawings of various mediums and has exhibited his artworks regionally in solo and group exhibitions in Maryland, Pennsylvania, New Jersey and New York City from the years 2002 to 2020. He has received the "Palmer Award for Excellence" at the Trenton City Museum at Ellarslie for his oil painting, "The Artist and his Model". His pastel paintings, "Butterfly Dance", "Reflection", and "Blossom", have been featured in *The Best of America Pastel Artists Volume II*. His oil painting, "The Artist and his Model", has also been published in the book, *Important World Artists Vol. I, A World of Art*.

He currently teaches various Fine Art classes on painting and drawing, live online and face-to-face, at several campuses of Bucks County Community College in Pennsylvania.

He is also a member of the national fine arts organizations, *Portrait Society of America*, *The Pastel Society of America*, and *Oil Painters of America*, and the local arts organizations in Bucks County, *Artsbridge*, *Artists of Yardley,* and *Artists of Bristol on the Delaware*. He has published two books on art-related topics - *Portrait and Nude*

Painting & Philosophies (2012) and *Interview between the Jackass and the Artist* (2013, Revised 2021), and is working on several other books on other art-related topics.

He is the CEO and Founder of Juno Arts Center Inc., a Pennsylvania corporation that produces and sells original artworks of its Founder, fine artwork prints, and art-related books. Copies of many of his original oil and pastel paintings and charcoal and pencil drawings are displayed in an online gallery at the website, https://www.normanfinearts.com/.

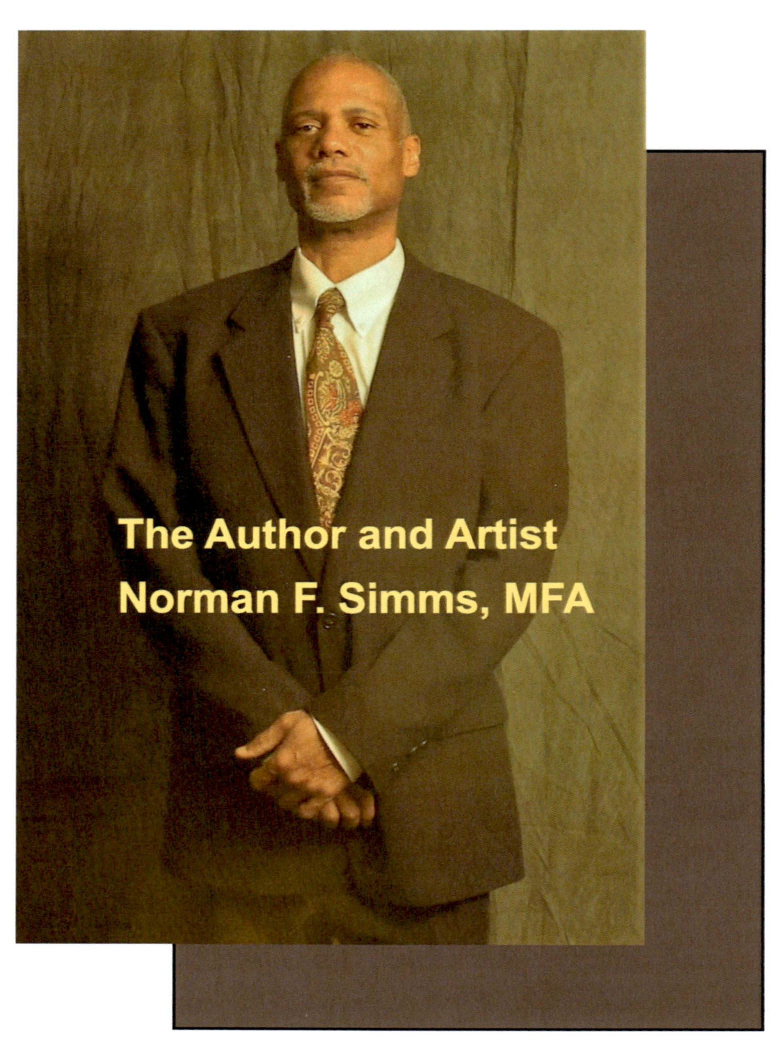

Preface

I feel that it is imperative for artists to continue exploring new ways to see and communicate ideas, to educate and expose the world to new beauties and viewpoints. Our job as artists is to entertain and enlighten our viewers. If you are like me and want to deliver a universal message, a message that states that life is a beautiful thing despite the bumps and unexpected twists we go through during life's journey, you will enjoy expanding that beauty by adding your creative drawings in a way that only you can. This is the purpose for writing this book. It is for you to achieve success, happiness, and joy in learning how to draw and create your own wonderful drawings.

Why We Draw?

We draw to stimulate our minds, as we must focus on planning, reasoning, movement, emotion and problem solving, whether it is a technical drawing or a landscape in our neighborhood. You have to activate your mind's visual processing and work with your perception, observation, and memory. This mind exercise creates a feeling of calmness as your mind develops a keen sense of focus. Drawing involves exploring various subjects and topics, including one's self visually in and out of this world. Drawing is more than just copying the subject matter; it is interpreting what you see and visually communicating the ideas and feelings that you personally relate to – referred to as self-expression.

Drawing is visual thinking – a way of exploring and understanding ideas and experiences as we record people, places, things, memories and events. Drawing is a record of existence and varies from each individual as each individual has a different life and experience, which creates different types and styles of marks on flat surfaces.

Scope

The material in this book series comes from many years of studying works of master artists and teaching important concepts that most accomplished artists have already mastered. Each lesson will explore new materials and techniques. Although times have historically changed some drawing methods, still a great deal of drawing methodologies and practices have stayed the same in making great drawings.

This book is a little more advanced than the first four books in this series and will introduce you to artist drawings and paintings with pastels. We will learn how to incorporate abstract in an artwork as we work in creating various line strokes, creating various textures, and experimenting with the pastels.

This book will help you transition from drawing to painting. If you apply what you already know about drawing, you will find that painting is fairly easy. Remember, that your goal is to create the best drawing that you can. From this point, the best way to learn is by doing. You will apply all the drawing practices we have focused on up to this point, but will see and experiment with color, as we explored, briefly with color pencils.

It is important to note that talent is a factor, but the most important element is practice. The student that is willing to work will improve significantly.

Learning to Draw

There are no right or wrong ways to draw, but after years of studies, I will approach drawing in a logical way, that will allow you to slowly build your technical, compositional and comprehensive skills. Remember that there are many ways to draw – as you visualize the world. You will learn to draw what you see and to draw conceptually. Some things I will not be able to teach, such as patience - try to take deep breaths, relax and enjoy the moment, feel free to make mistakes, experiment to expand your visual and drawing vocabulary. In completing this book and others in the series, you should:

• Think of the big picture rather than parts – work on the entire composition at the same time.

• Observe relationships between forms and all negative and positive spaces.

• Create a focal point by emphasizing some elements and deemphasizing others.

• Arrange the composition to guide the viewer through the pictorial journey of shapes and space.

• Create a work of fine art that you and others will enjoy looking at.

Understanding Drawing and How it is Taught

I would like to welcome you to drawing, a practice used to visually communicate concepts, ideas or emotions. Drawing is a combination of straight and/or curved lines that represent thought. This thought is able to express ideas, directions, feelings, or a combination of all of these visually.

There are three general categories of creating representative drawings: technical drawings, sometimes referred to as design drawings, physical observation/realistic or Atelier drawings, and imaginative drawings, where memory is extensively used.

Teaching Methods for Learning to Draw

Academy setting (workshop or studio) is where a professional artist (master) and his or her students are in the most ideal environment for the apprentices to grow as artists. This is because they receive instant feedback. The academy setting has become popular because it is presented in the form of standardized learning, additional tips, and learning from several sources. The academy setting is necessary due to larger numbers of students and the time constraints of both the student and the master.

Technical or design drawings consist of multi-view drawings; a related set of orthographic projections. Each projection reveals a particular aspect of an object. Together, they are able to fully describe the object in both 2-dimensional and 3-dimensional forms.

Orthographic projection uses views to project adjacent views perpendicular to the picture plane. These views are 2-dimensional. To create a sense of depth to 2-dimensional images, we need to know their height, width, and depth. In fine art, we use perspective and foreshortening to depict 3-dimensional subjects and distance.

Perspective is a technique for depicting volumes and relationships of depth on a flat surface. There are aerial, linear, and foreshortening perspectives. In technical drawings, linear perspective is used and assumes the viewer sees through a single eye.

People with two eyes almost never see anything in this way. We constantly scan, collect, manipulate, and process data to form our perception and understanding of the visual world. Still linear perspective is a valuable tool and can give the observer the feel of a 3-dimensional world.

Technical drawings are created by measurement only. Their purpose is to have manufacturers, builders, or site planners use these drawings as an accurate guide to making components, products, architectural or site plans for laying out plans from these drawings. Today these drawings are usually done on a computer using CAD (Computer Aided Design) softwares.

Physical observation drawings are mental examinations of forms and shapes relationships. Art instructors will often hear the statement: “I can’t draw”. This statement is not totally true, but neither is it totally false. Masterful drawing is a combination of work and knowledge. You need to have a sound foundation of the fundamentals and draftsmanship or skill of drawing, without using any aids. Mastering the draftsmanship of drawing is like learning to add, subtract, and multiply, without using a calculator. When you can place a line exactly where you want it, and when you can draw a shape exactly as you see or choose to interpret it, then you have become skilled at drawing.

We use our eyes and brain to subconsciously see distorted realisms. This is the reason it is difficult for many to accurately draw. Drawing is problematic for some beginners, partly for the reason that everything we see is interpreted by the mind, and everyone’s mind has some pre-established patterns of how things should look. In other words, we don’t always really see what’s in front of us. Nevertheless, we fall back on the images in our mind. People who have trouble drawing keep relying on these memorized pictures in their minds that prevent their eyes from seeing the true shapes, colors, and textures of things they draw.

Drawing is more than a mere representation of something before the viewer. It is a series of inviting or defensive marks. If you approach drawing not knowing the "why" behind the madness that dominates the viewer, then your skills are also lacking. Remember the general purpose of drawing is to communicate.

Even as a hobbyist, it is frustrating to rely on luck to communicate your thoughts, emotions, and energy to your viewers.

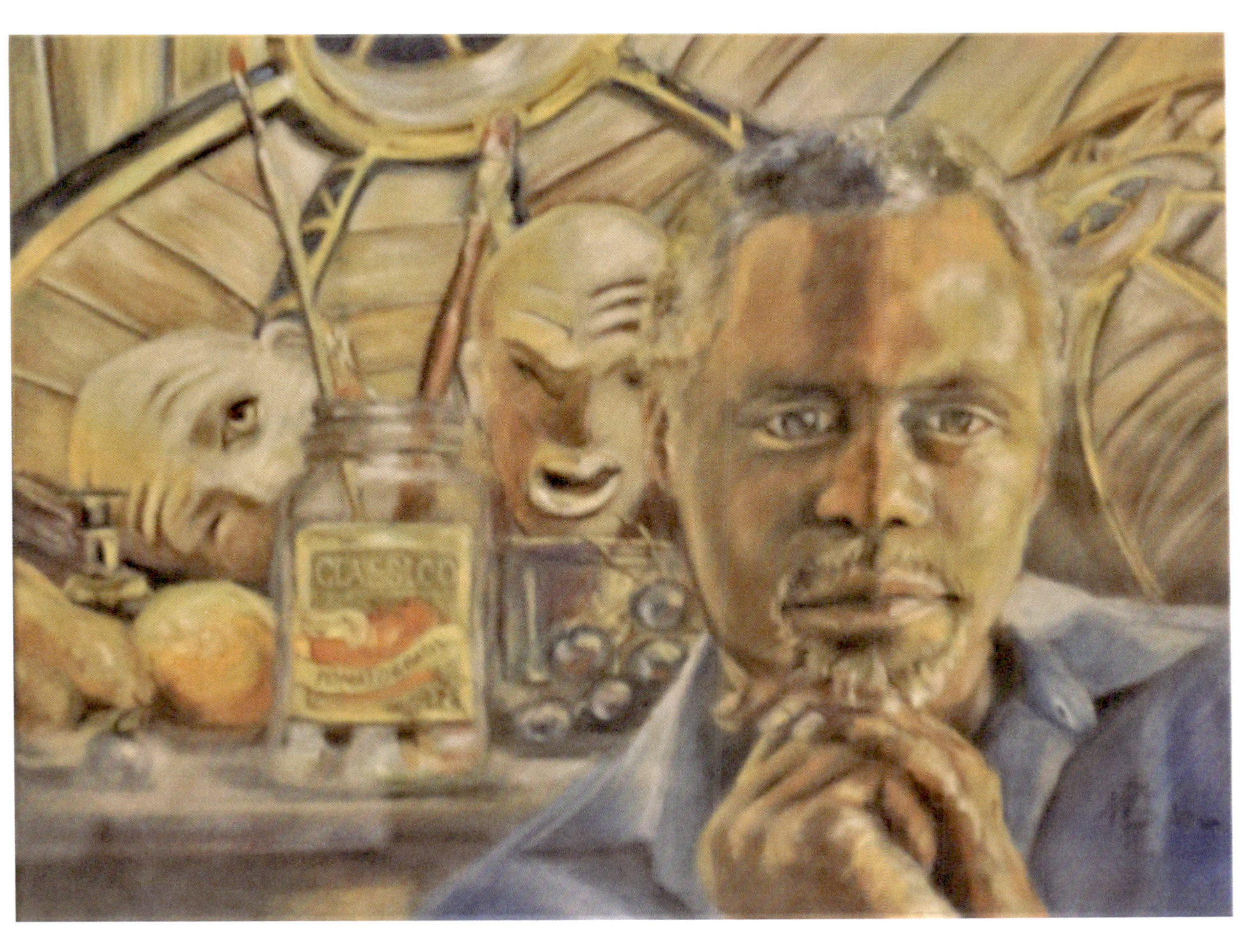

"Art Lover" Pastel on pastel board, 2006

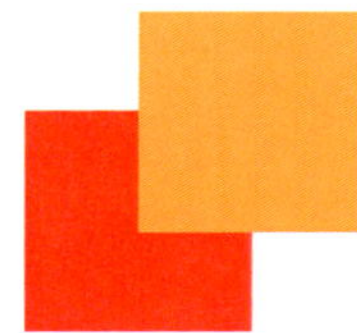

BOOK FIVE
TABLE OF CONTENTS
Drawing and Painting with Pastels

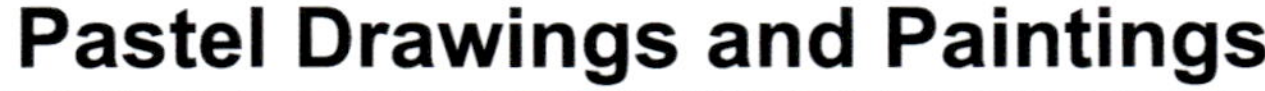

Pastel Drawings and Paintings

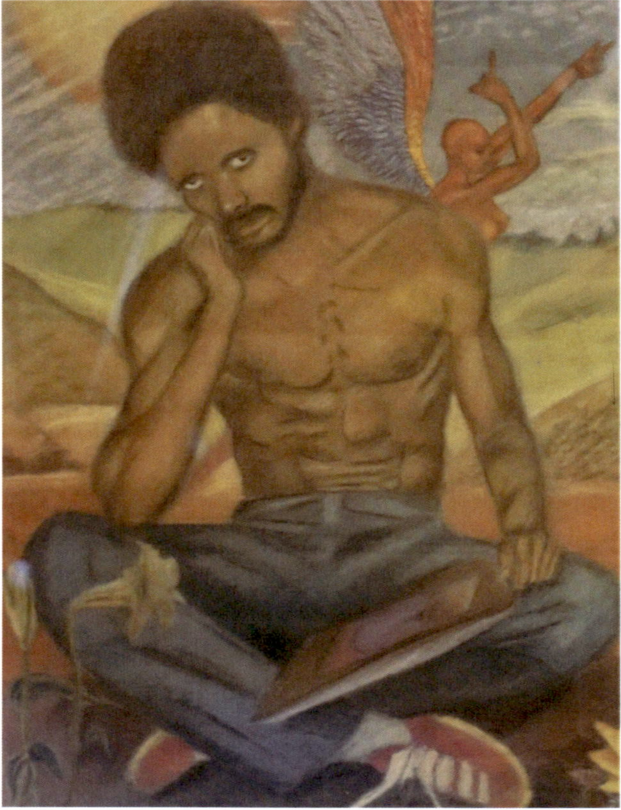

"The Dreamer" Pastel on pastel paper, 1977

Working with Pastels

I did one of my first pastels painting in 1975 for a school drawing assignment at Murray State University. I named the painting "The Dreamer". When the instructor looked at the pastel artwork, he said to me: "Is this a painting or a drawing?" I looked at it and I did not know what to say. Now I understand the difference between pastel drawings and pastel paintings. However, before I explain this difference, let's get a general understanding of what pastels are.

All mediums (Watercolors, Oil Paints, Pastels, etc.) consist of a pigment and a binder. Pastels are held like a pencil or a stick of charcoal. There are 4 categories that pastels come in: hard pastels, soft pastels, pastel pencils, and oil pastels. All forms of pastels can be used together, with the exception of oil pastels. Oil pastels are bound with oil and wax so they will not blend with hard pastels and soft pastels. The hardness or softness of the pastel is determined by the amount of binder in the stick. Hard pastel has more binder and less pigment. Soft pastel has less binder and more pigment. Soft pastels easily smudge and blend. Hard pastels are good for creating tight details. The pastel pencil will give the artist more control over detailed areas.

Pastels are great at blending, and are able to create luscious textures that give a rich "painterly" appearance to an artwork. When the artwork surface area is entirely covered in pastel, the artwork is considered a painting. When the artwork surface area is not fully covered in pastel and a noticeable amount of surface area is showing through, the artwork is considered a drawing.

Artists can achieve luscious, textured, rich colors with pastels, and they don't need a lot of tools to work with as in other painting mediums. Artists working with pastels must be aware of the tiny dust particles floating into the air from pastels. Therefore, make sure you have proper ventilation in the room where you are working with pastels. You may even want to wear a face mask. Inhaled pastel dust particles can cause serious health problems. Sparingly use only workable fixative spray on the pastel artwork, but be aware that this may dull and darken the colors on this artwork. Also, remember that fixative sprays are toxic, so they should be used outdoors on the pastel artwork.

Finally, pastels pigments are not permanently fixed to the artwork surface, so you must handle the pastel artwork extra carefully. Pastel artwork can accidentally smudge or be easily damaged. Be very careful with your pastel artworks.

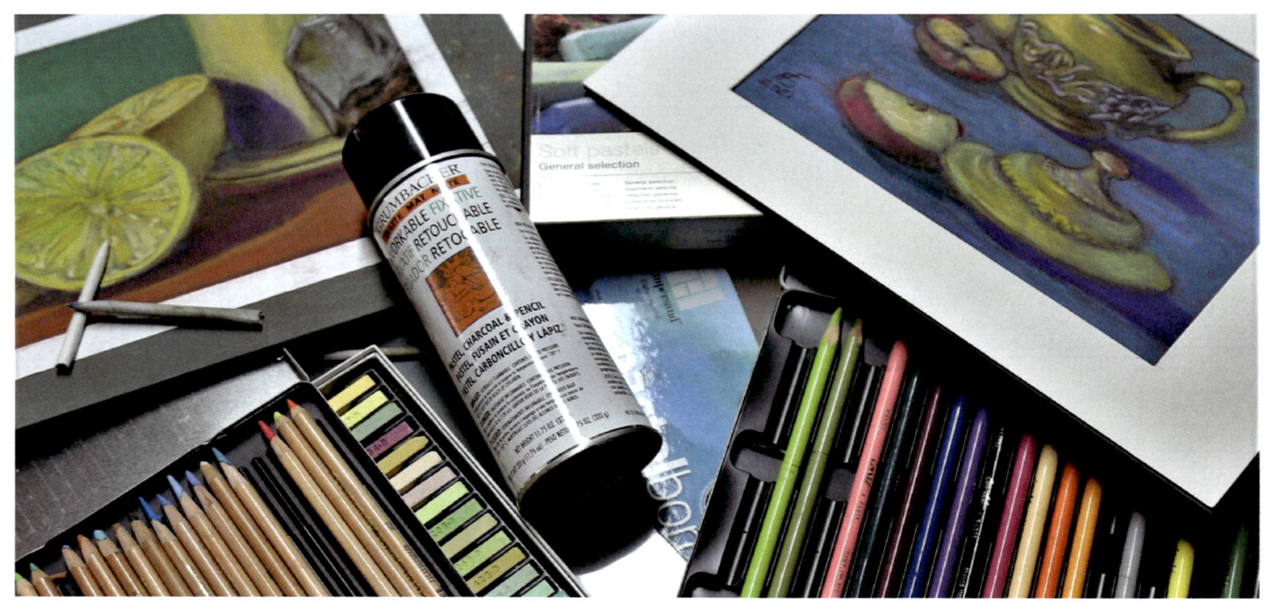

Pastel as an Artist Medium

Pastels have been used by many of the top artists throughout the history of the art world. Pastels have produced many of the world's most beautiful artworks by some of the most famous artists, such as **Edgar Degas**, who worked with pastels as his primary medium, often combining it with other mediums such as watercolors and oil in the 1880s; **Jean François Millet**, who used pastels and explored using broken strokes of color, rather than blending the colors as many early pastelists did; and **Mary Cassatt**, who made her living as a pastel portrait artist living in Paris. Note the advantages of pastels – this medium can be manipulated with greater speed and ease than other mediums; it has no odor, and allows for frequent interruptions. There are many more pastelists artists that I could name, including myself. I have always been drawn to this medium because I was always attracted to the rich colors of pastels. If you are reading this, I hope you are thinking about how this medium could be a way that you will be exploring your art and showing off your artistic skills in making it uniquely your own.

Tools and Materials for Pastels

Artists need the appropriate tools to create magnificent artworks. It is inspirational for artists that draw regularly to know that they have the right materials and tools on hand. Some pastels products will provide vibrant colors that later fade away. As a serious artist, you will want to avoid such a problem. The features of your pastels should be lightfastness, that is resistant to fading when exposed to light, and radiant in colors. Pressing too hard on the paper material with pastels may ruin the integrity of the material surface. Note that artist grade pastels have a much higher quality and are significantly different from student grade pastels. There are many factors to consider in selecting the ideal materials and tools for your needs. As you begin to work with several selections of various pastels and materials, you will know what works best with your particular style.

Pastel Pencils

The various types of professional pastel pencils can produce very different results. We will include Stabilo CarbOthello Pastel Pencils, Faber-Bastell Pitt Pastel Pencils, Derwent Pastel Pencils, Conté á Paris Pastel Pencils, and Caran D'ache Pastel Pencils.

When purchasing your pastel pencils, pricing is a factor. However, don't look for untested cheaper pastel substitutes because these alternative pastel brands do not deliver and perform as the professional brands do. The alternative pastel brands may have duller colors, use synthetic materials, and can't maintain fine points.

Try and select a pastel brand that sells the pastel pencils individually. The advantage to doing this is that you can test an individual pastel pencil or replace a pastel color cheaper than purchasing a whole set of pastel pencils in order to replace a few pastel colors. Finally, pastel pencils sets, unlike hard and soft pastels sets, are limited in the selections of colors. If you work with a lot of detail within your artwork, you may want to see if your pastel brand has a larger selection of colors. Sets may come in 12, 24, 36, 48, and 60 packages. Remember to check if you can purchase each individual pastel individually.

Hard Pastels

There are a number of good hard pastels sets out on the market. This type of pastel is easier to control than soft pastels. The **Prismacolor 27051 Set** contains 96 different shades, extraordinary color saturation, and great blending capacity. The **Faber-Castell Polychromos Set** has 36 vibrant smudge-proof shades. The **Cretacolor Pastel Carré Hard Pastel Set** has 72 vibrant shades which are easy to blend shades that do not leave dusty residues and can be used with wet media. **The Mungyo Gallery Semi-Hard Pastels Set** is a 36 set of high-quality, environment-friendly, rich pigmentation shades and creates less dusty material.

Soft Pastels

The **Rembrandt Soft Pastels** from Royal Talens is the professional pastelists choice. They will never lose their luster during your lifetime. The **Sennelier Soft Pastels** are great, but don't provide much of a savings cost wise. The cost of a Sennelier pastel stick is about $5.00 each. A Sennelier set of 525-piece pastel sticks of all their colors would be over $1,000. They provide beautiful results; however, if you are working on a budget, this may be an overkill. The **Blick Artists Soft Pastels**, like the Sennelier Soft Pastels and the Rembrandt Soft Pastels, will produce extremely vibrant and bright colors, but at a more affordable price, and they are available individually and as a set.

Pan Pastels

PanPastels are a form of soft pastels that have less binder and higher pigment concentration, are low in dust, and are placed in a pan or jar. The Colorfin company is the creator of PanPastel colors. PanPastels are easier and less messy to use. PanPastels can be applied with a Sofft tool, which is a dense micropore sponge that comes in a variety of sizes.

Surfaces and Support for Pastel Artworks

When selecting a surface for applying pastels, you need a surface with **tooth and texture** for the pastel to grip to and shave the pigment from the pastel sticks. Your surface should be able to take some rubbing and blending. Pastel surfaces should have enough tooth to accept multiple **layers** of pastel. Select a surface with less tooth if you want precise **details** and hard lines and edges, or you know you will be blending colors.

Paper texture is important and also must be tough enough to withstand the rubbing, blending, and erasing frequently used in pastels works. The strongest papers are made from 100% cotton (rag paper), which is acid-free and has been treated to prevent it from yellowing over time. It is common for pastel artists to use toned color paper when using a limited range of pastel colors.

Pastel paper (Ingres paper) is texture paper that comes in a wide range of colors and tones. Some common pastel surfaces are Canson Mi-Teintes Drawing Paper, Canson Mi-Teintes Touch Sanded Papers and Boards, Canson Ingres Drawing Papers, Art Spectrum Colourfix Coated Pastel Paper, Hahnemuhle Bugra Pastel Paper, Strathmore 400 Series Pastel Pads, Richeson Premium Pastel Surfaces, and Ampersand Pastel Board.

Fixative (Workable)

Due to the nature of pastel dust, not using a fixative can be a problem, and at the same time, improperly using a fixative can be a safely risk when used incorrectly. Artists use pastel by adding layers of pastel over one another. A light coat of **workable fixative** will help to generate a tooth that will allow the pastel to latch onto the surface effortlessly. Soft pastels are dusty and chalky and easily fall off the surface. Spraying a light coat of workable fixative on a pastel artwork will ensure that the pastel retains its detail and brilliance. There are fixative that are designed for pastels and has key preservation qualities, such as Sennelier pastel fixative. Remember to spray your pastel artwork outside where it is well ventilated.

Pastel Blending Tools

It is common for artists to blend pastels with their **fingers**. The problems with doing this are that many surfaces may turn your fingers raw after continuing to rub for an extended amount of time; you will not be able to blend smaller areas without smudging other areas of your artwork; and you will need to wash your hands frequently to avoid transferring colors to other areas of your artwork.

Pastel shapers (color shapers) have flat or tapered rubbery ends. The pointy tapered pastel shapers are useful for blending small areas or working with fine detail, while the flat pastel shapers are good for blending larger areas.

Holbein pastel brushes come in a variety of shapes and are specifically designed for blending pastels.

Tortillons, also referred to as stumps, are tightly wound sheets of paper. You simply rub the tortillon on the area you want to blend. When the tortillon gets too dirty, simply unwind the paper to expose a fresh tip.

Chamois is a type of super soft and flexible leather that is excellent for blending colors with pastels. Make sure you use a chamois that is specifically designed for artists. Note: There are chamois designed for shining cars which are not used by artists.

The **kneaded rubber** is also great for blending tiny area pastels.

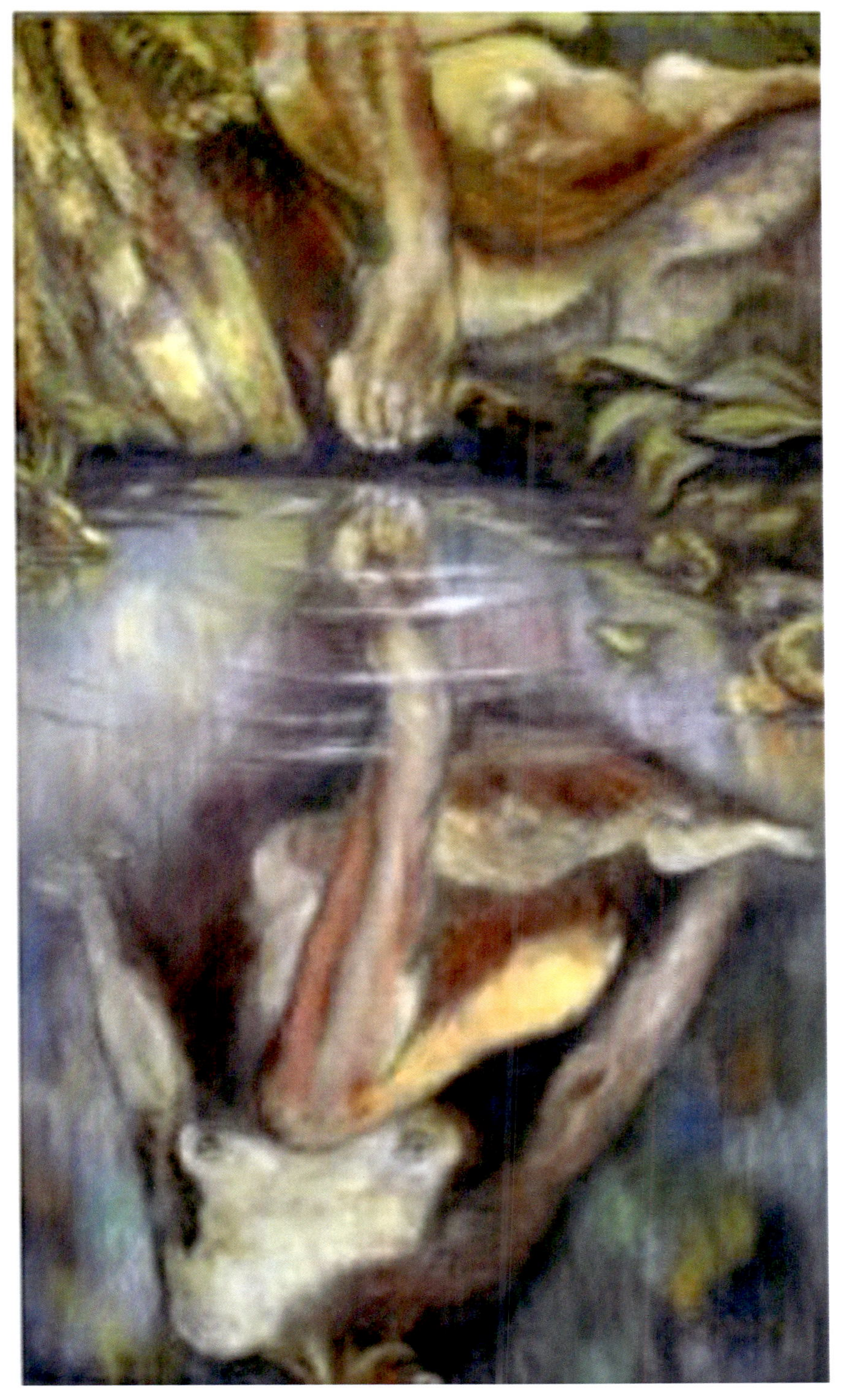

"Reflecting Pond" Pastel on pastel board, 2007

Supplies Needed for this Book

1. Journal: Notebook and sketchbook.

The Journal is your individual written responses to focus questions, artist notes, and ideas preliminary sketches.

2. Drafting/Masking tape or clips.

3. Drawing Surface (tinted pastels or charcoal paper and 11 X 14-inch pastel board.

4. Pastels: Hard (nu-pastels), pencils, and/or soft non-oil pastels.

5. Charcoal: Assortment of compressed and vine.

6. Conté crayons: Black, brown, and white.

7. Portfolio Cover: Cardboard or plastic case for drawings.

The Portfolio is a collection of your drawings. All work should be signed, dated and cleanly presented.

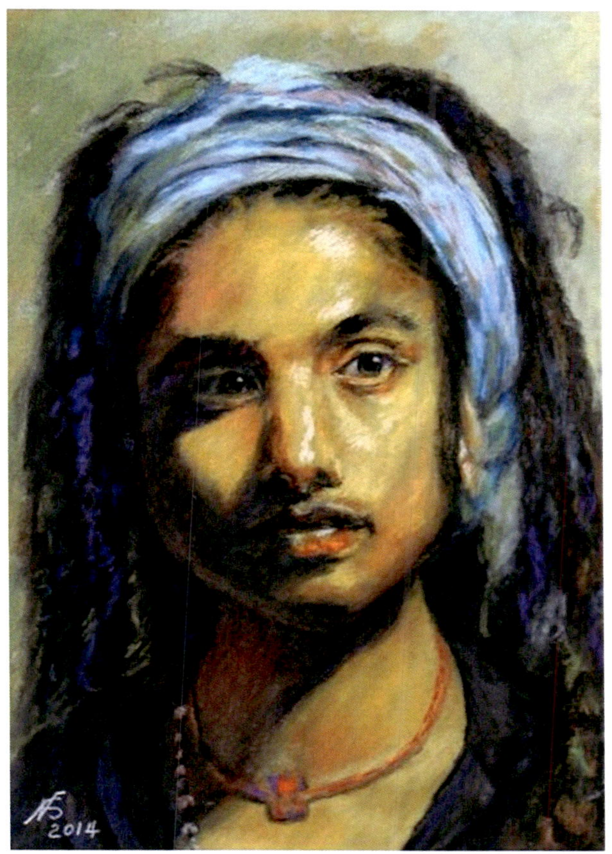

"Young Woman" Pastel on pastel board, 2014

Drawing and Painting with Pastels

The Painting "Young Woman" was created using pastels. The benefits of working with the pastel medium are:

1. Paintings are relatively easy to transport to various locations, provided you have a proper portfolio case;

2. Pastels are an excellent choice for sketching, drawing, and painting your subject or scene; and

3. You can produce deep, rich luscious colors and velvety textures and are able to blend splendid luminosity colors.

Introduction to Pastels - Focus Questions 1

What are Pastels?

Pastels are an art medium consisting of pure powdered pigment and a binder.

How permanent are pastels?

Pastels are permanent and can last just as long as any other medium. Pastels never crack, yellow, or darken over time.

What are the types of pastels?

Most common types are hard, soft, and oil. Hard pastels are made from the same ingredients as soft pastels, except they contain more binder and less pigment. This means that their colors are not as intense, but they don't crumble or break as easily. Oil pastels contain oil and cannot be mixed with hard pastels or soft pastels.

What are Values referring to in Art?

Value is the lightness or darkness of a color or tone that we see on objects when light is projected onto it. Light reflects off objects into our eyes and our minds interpret that light and rationalize what we see.

Why are Values important?

Values are the key to the illusion of form in realistic artworks.

What do Shapes mean in the world of Art?

Shapes are areas where their boundaries are enclosed by lines, values, colors, or textures. Shapes create the illusion of three-dimensional form when adding values correctly to them.

What is Chiaroscuro?

Chiaroscuro is what you may refer to as shading. It is an Italian word describing the effect of contrasting areas of light and dark in an artwork.

What do you think of the Artist Edgar Degas?

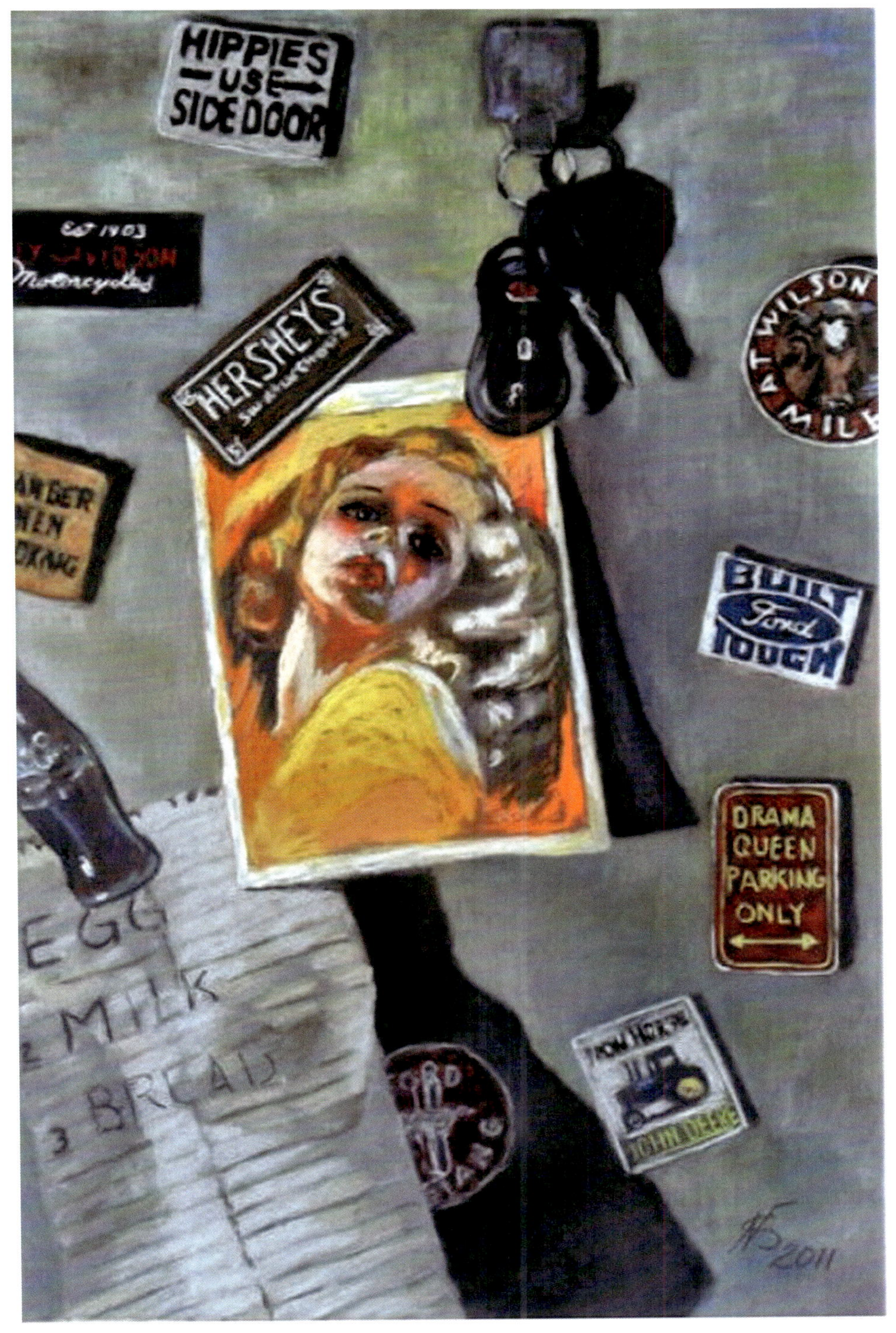

"Refrigerator Magnets and Post Card" Pastel on pastel board, 2007

I. Working with Still Life with Pastels

Pastels give the artist the best of both the drawing experience and the painting experience. Depending on how you apply this dry medium, the finished product could be considered a drawing or a painting. You are able to apply layers over previous applications and mix the colors as if it was paint. Pastels are similar to charcoal drawing, but require a greater understanding of colors and additions to value relationships.

The paper plays an important role in the success and the performance of your artwork. Paper should have enough tooth to accept a number of layers and marks to be applied to the paper used.

Learning to work with pastel is like learning to drive a car. I can tell you how to drive a car, but it is best to have you sit behind the wheel and experience it. So, be patience with yourself; draw, paint and enjoy working with pastels.

Drawing Review

So far, we learned about the various pastels mediums and supplies used to create pastels drawings and paintings. We also experimented with arranging a still life composition by adding a light source and placing objects in interesting arrangements. We spent time drawing what we have arranged in previous books.

We discovered that a common mistake made when students are creating symmetrical objects is drawing the ellipse incorrectly. We will learn how to use a horizontal center line to create symmetrical objects correctly. We learn the important of drawing the ellipses correctly. A circle that is viewed from the side will be drawn as an ellipse. An ellipse has a major axis and a minor axis, which are 90 degrees to each other. An incorrectly drawn ellipse is a common mistake that beginners encounter in their artworks. Common errors are making a sausage shape or drawing pointed ends on the ellipse.

What did you think of the **Artist** Edgar Degas? Did you like Degas' work? Why? If you don't like his work, why not? What do you think when viewing his work?

Creating Composition (Arrangements) for Still Life

First: Select a Format and a Viewpoint.

The first compositional decision you will make is the outer format. The shape and size of your artwork will communicate a mood. So often students will start their artworks with whatever size paper that is available and fit the composition within the allotted space. Selecting your outer format is one thing that cannot be changed once the artwork begins, so it is important that you choose your outer format to help you to communicate your emotional intent.

Experiment with various formats – horizontal and vertical, large and small.

In making your selections and observations about formats, take notes on how the format affects your mood.

Look at the various formats and arrangements of the Still-Life on the following pages.

Second: Breathe life into your composition by making small changes below to the arrangement:

a. Create interesting negative spaces and positive spaces in your composition.
b. Add different textures and scales for the objects.
c. Create a wider tonal range of values.
d. Include shadows as part of your composition.

Direct the Viewer's eye through the composition.

Create a variety of shapes, and arrange the objects in a way that moves the Viewer's eye through the artwork.

Draw ellipse edges correctly. (No pointy edges or flat sides).

Understanding Compositional Arrangements

Note: The same arrangements viewed and cropped in various ways.

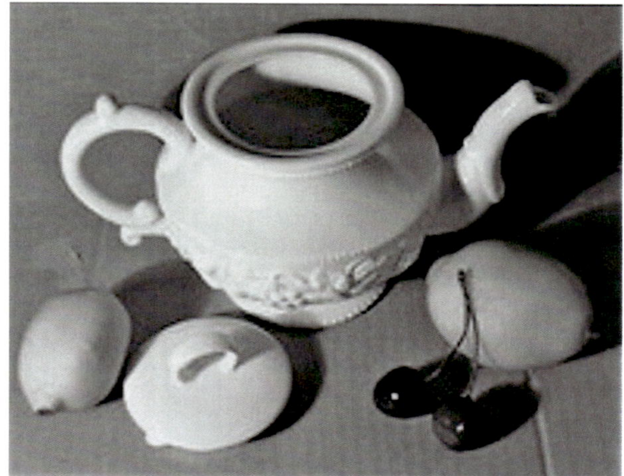

LARGE: majestic, magnificent, awe-inspiring, impressive, generous, expansive, loud, exuberant, liberating, spacious, vast, bulky, weighty, and voluminous.

MEDIUM: comfortable and adaptable.

SMALL: intimate, delicate, limited, modest, humble, and quiet.

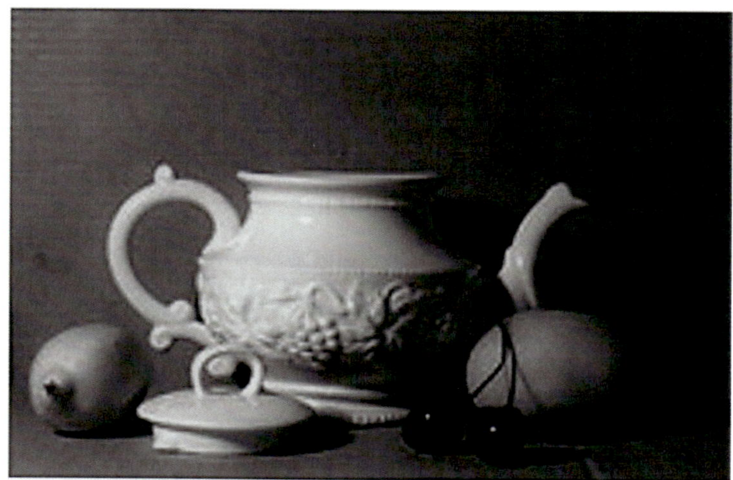

STANDARD SIZES SHAPE: (example, 18 inches x 24 inches) comfortable, adaptable, moderate, stable, calm, graceful, and nonassertive.

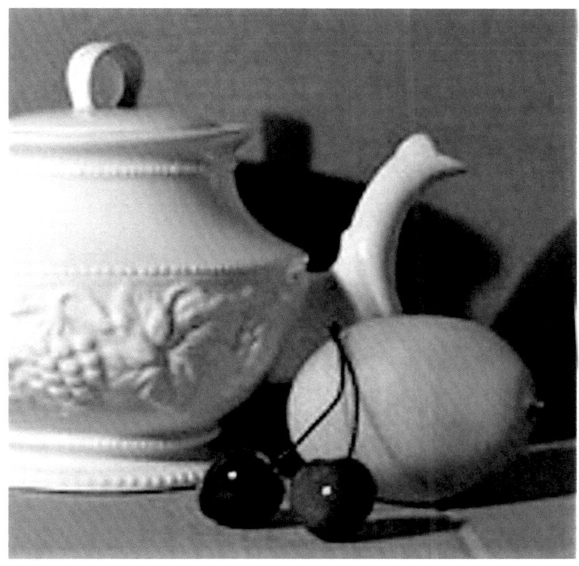

SQUARE: (example, 20 inches x 20 inches) solid, blunt, stark, angular, strong, straightforward, firm, formal, rigid, and direct.

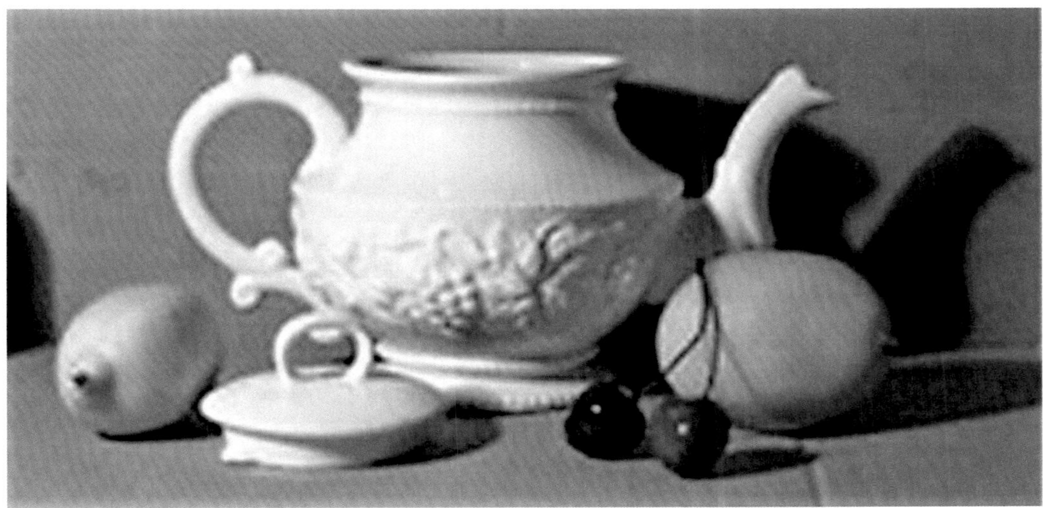

VERTICAL: (example, 24 inches x 12 inches) dramatic, exaggerated, tall, upright, powerful, confident, authoritative, influential, energetic, tense, strong, and forceful.

HORIZONTAL: (example, 12 inches x 24 inches) dramatic, exaggerated, precarious, secure, balanced, reclining, restful, and panoramic.

Creating Successful Paintings

Still life depicts inanimate objects that will include flowers, fruit, and other nonliving items carefully arranged to create specific visual effects. Landscapes usually depict mountains, valleys, trees, rivers, clouds, and forests, to name a few subjects. Portraiture and anatomy in art will show creative expression of the structural form of life. The artist's task is to arrange the main subject with its other elements into a coherent composition. Planning to create a painting will require the artist to first, select a subject to paint; second, find what you want the viewer to focus on; and third, decide where to locate the focal area. In short, the artist has to make many decisions and solve many problems that will enable the artist to begin and to complete the artwork.

Whether working from imagination, or a reference photograph, or life, the artist must still determine how to represent the subject matter. I can show you several ways that I would create a landscape using pastels. However, when it comes to you as an individual creating art, there are no rules or one particular way to approach your artwork.

I will show you a few methods and materials that you can use, but it is up to each individual artist to experiment and rely on himself or herself to learn to work as he or she wishes. Art is one of the few activities that will give you, as an artist, the freedom to create and express yourself.

Thinking like an Artist in creating Artworks

1. What and why are you going to Paint this Subject?

Your desire to create art comes from inspiration within you. Having a sketchbook for sketching and taking notes in a sketchbook about what you see allow you to experiment with various subjects, colors, values and compositions.

You should create artwork that excites you. Your goal should not be to only copy subjects. Your goal should be to express and add your personal feelings and passion when painting subjects in your artwork.

2. What Size will your Artwork be?

Size can create drama or emphasize subjects. Size can also aid in creating certain moods. For the beginner working with a new medium, I suggest working with a smaller, no larger than 11" x 14", surface. This small size will give the artist time to experiment and create an artwork in a reasonable time and use very little of the medium on each project.

3. What Shapes, Lines and Values are you Going to Use in Establishing your Artwork Composition?

Shapes are just areas that could be realistic or abstract. The edges of the shapes are lines and create the artwork's composition. The background - negative space - is also a shape. Plan your artwork by making studies and sketches and arranging the larger shapes' masses. Within these masses, show the positions of the light areas and dark areas referred to as Value studies. The use of lines, shapes, colors, and values in the arrangement is essential for your artwork to be successful.

4. What will be your Focal Point(s)? Where will your Focal Point(s) be Located? How will you Highlight the Focal Point(s)?

An artwork needs at least one focal point, which is the area of the artwork's major interest and where the eye of the viewer should be drawn. It is common for artists to place a few secondary elements of interest in an artwork in order to allow the eye of the viewer to move around the artwork.

Avoid placing the focal point in the middle of your artwork, (both horizontally or vertically) in your artwork, or too close to the edges of your artwork. The focal point is usually where the highest value contrast is located and the sharpest edges are.

5. What Colors, Techniques, and Textures will you Include in your Artwork?

Artists should be able to create feeling or perception within their artwork. This is done by manipulating various elements of art (*i.e.*, color, temperature, shapes, lines, textures, values) within your artwork to create certain emotions associated with your artwork.

This is fully explored in Book Six of this series.

Demo Still Life 1

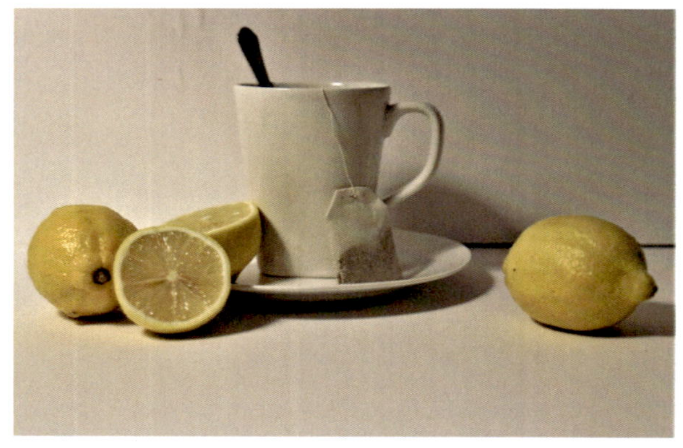

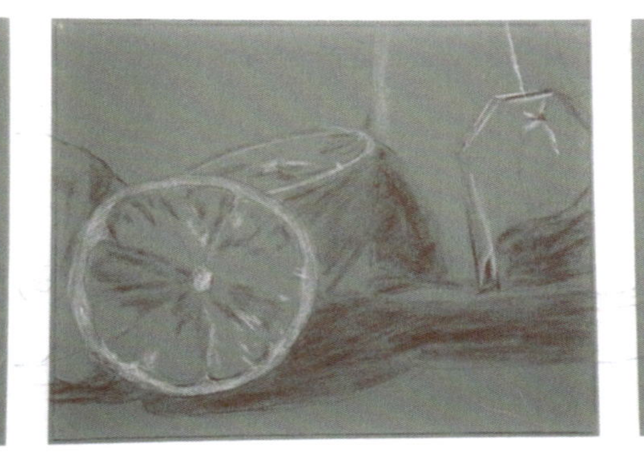

Reference Photo **Pastel Board Layout**

The Reference Photo - This composition has many possibilities. For my pastel work, I will crop this layout to focus in on the lemon and the teabag. I will also use a complementary color arrangement of red and green.

Pastel Board Layout - I am working on a 11" x 14" pastel board. I place drafting tape around the inside for a 9-1/2" x 7-1/2" border. This will allow spacing to place a Mat over the picture once it is completed.

I use black charcoal pencil and white pastel pencil to draw the lights and shadows of the composition. I cropped the reference photo in order to focus on the lemon and the tea bag.

Add Color - Add color to the composition. Add less detail to the objects that are farther away.

Add highlights - Give the artwork a name - "Lemon Tea", Sign and Date the work.

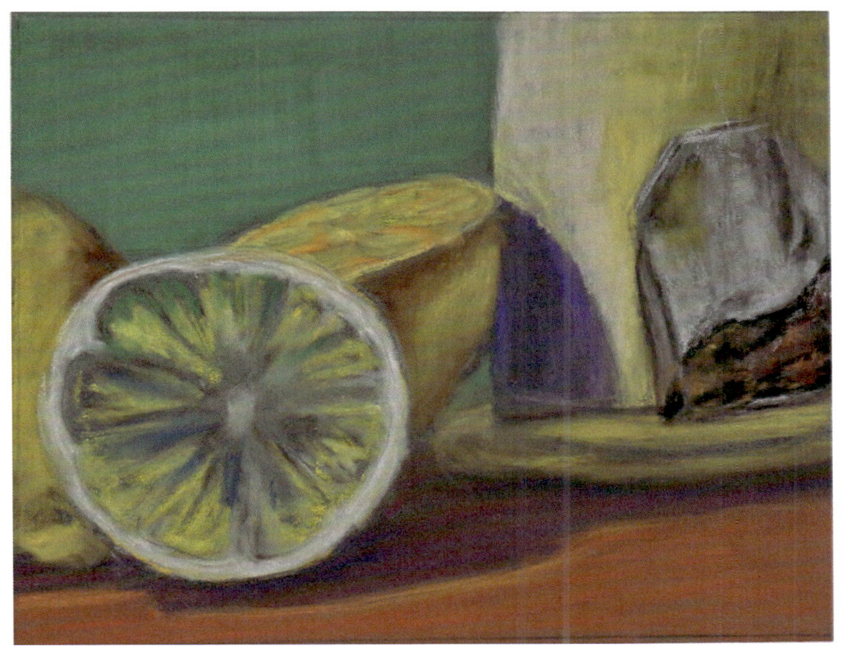

Add Color

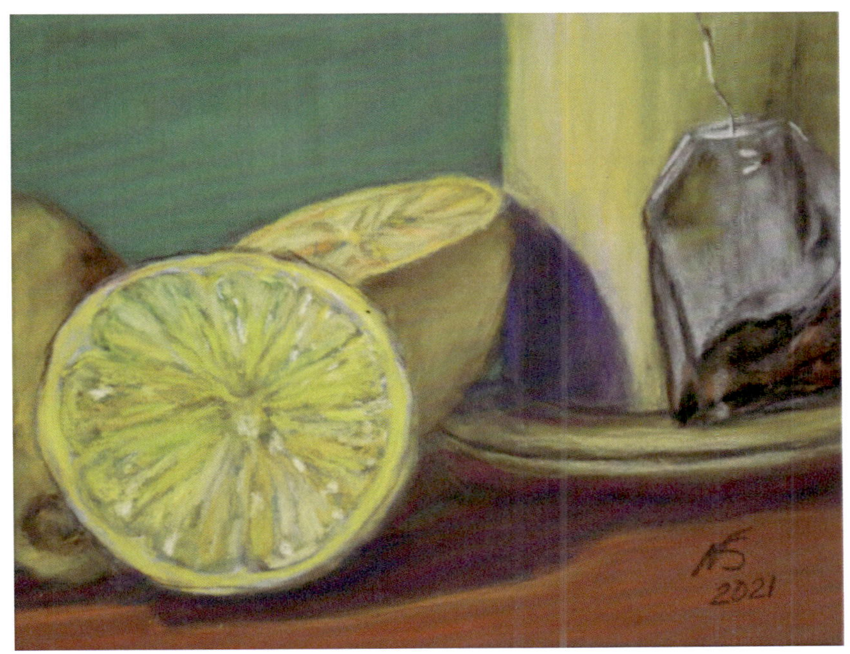

Add highlights

Demo Still Life 2

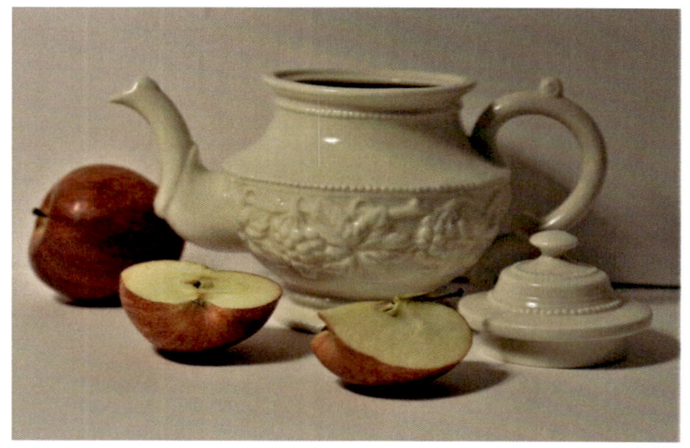

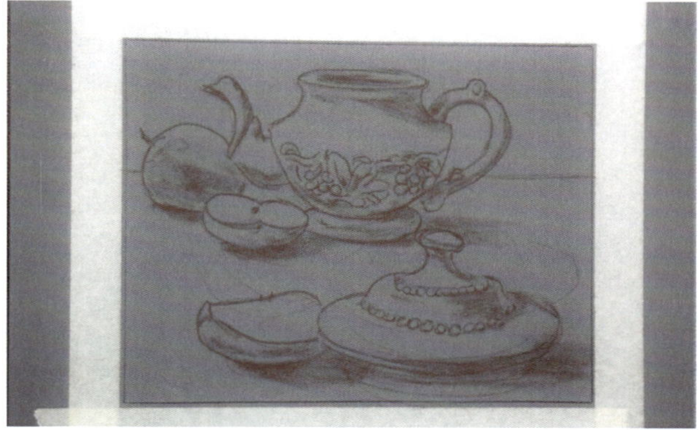

Reference Photo **Pastel Board Layout**

The Reference Photo - I like this composition, but I am going to bring the teapot top forward to create two separate units.

Pastel Board Layout - I am working on a 11” x 14″ pastel board. I place drafting tape around the inside for a 9-1/2” x 7-1/2″ border. This will allow spacing to place a Mat over the picture once it is completed. I drew my objects with charcoal pencil and white pastel pencil at this stage.

I use charcoal and pastel pencils to draw the lights and shadows of the composition. I increased the size and placed the object further down in the picture to indicate that these objects were in front (closer to the viewer).

Add Color - Add color to the composition. The color scheme is an analogous split complementary. I used the apple and the apple slices to direct my viewers' eyes into and through the picture.

Add highlights - Give the artwork a name - "Apple Slices", Sign and Date the work.

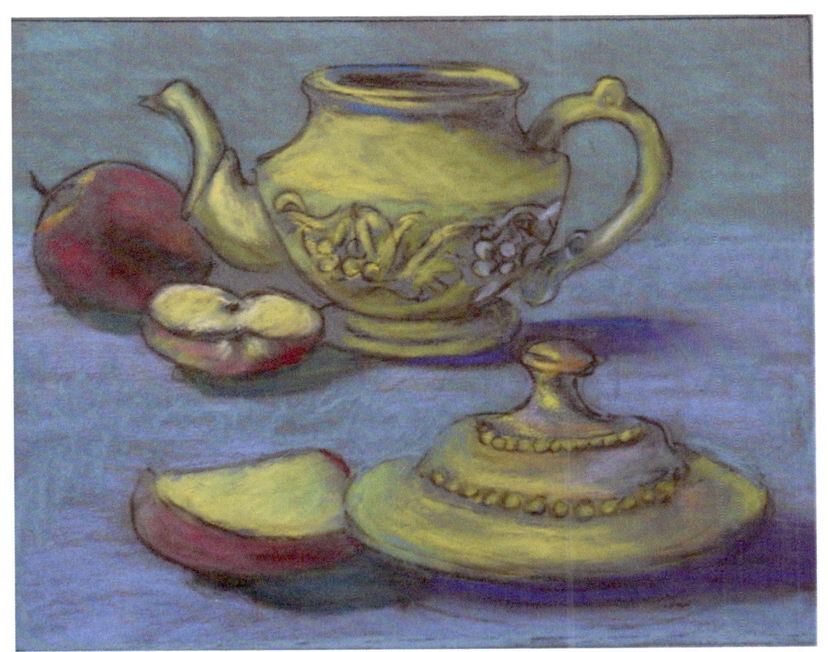

Add Color

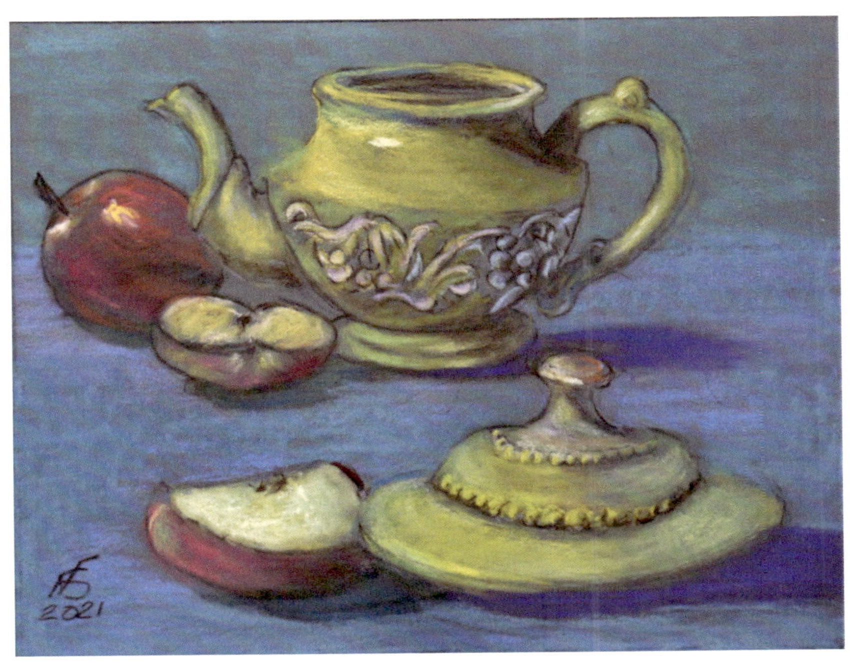

Add highlights

Assignment: BK 5-01 Still Life

Use at least one of the compositions to draw and add color using pastels. You may enlarge the drawings above the reference photos and use them as Templates.

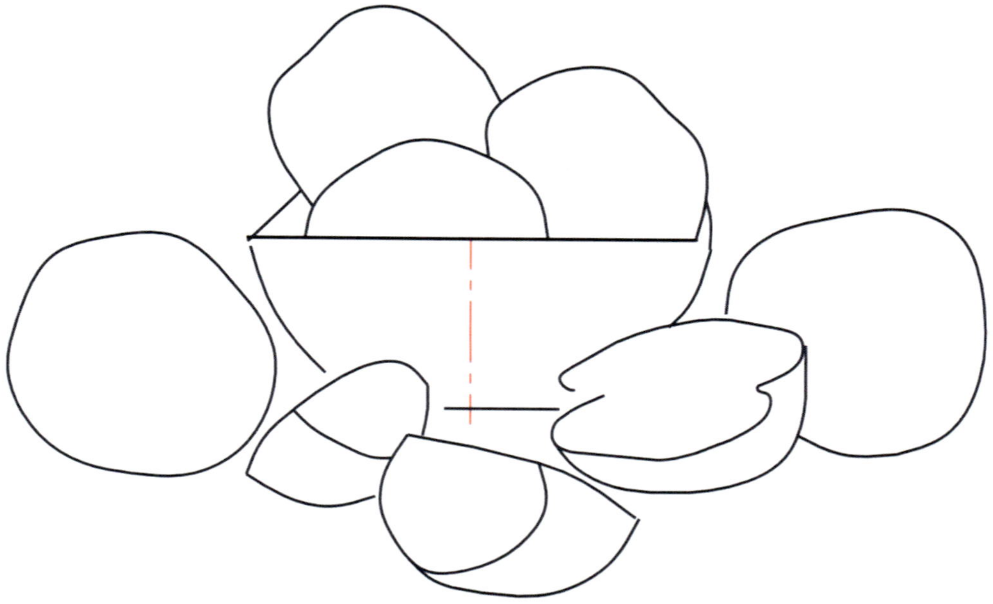

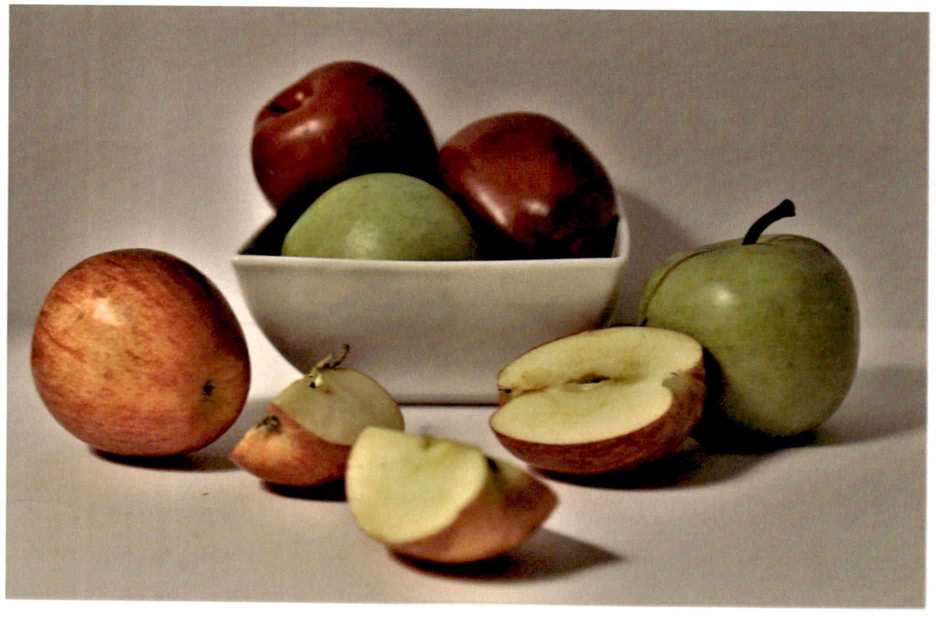

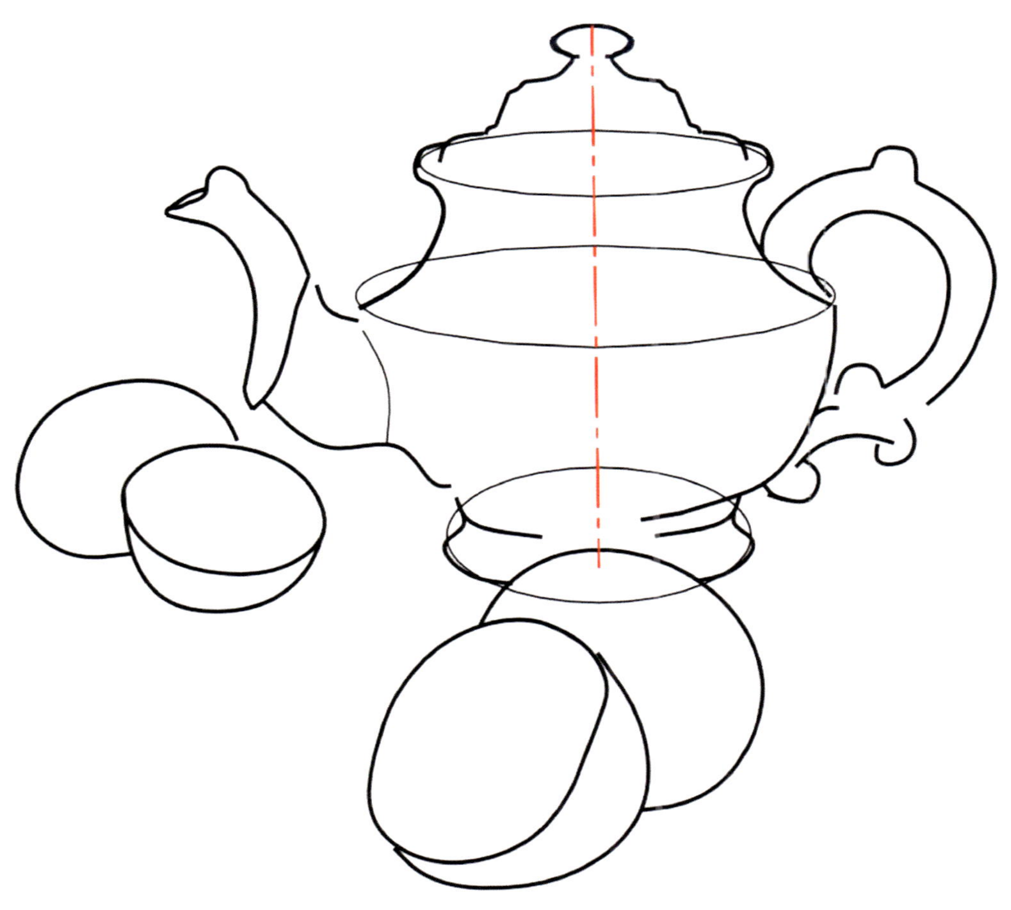

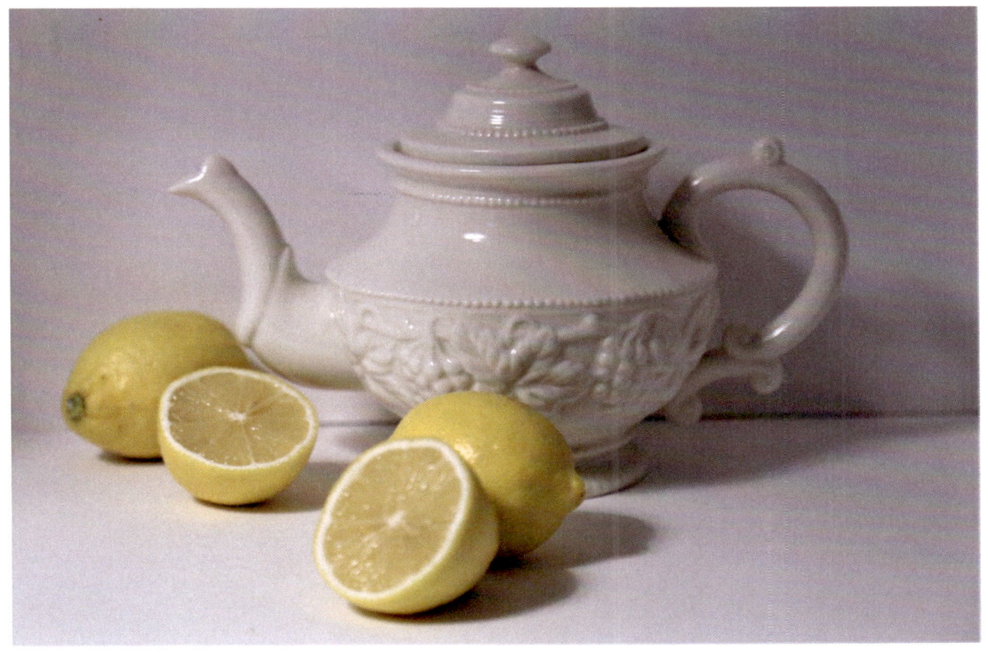

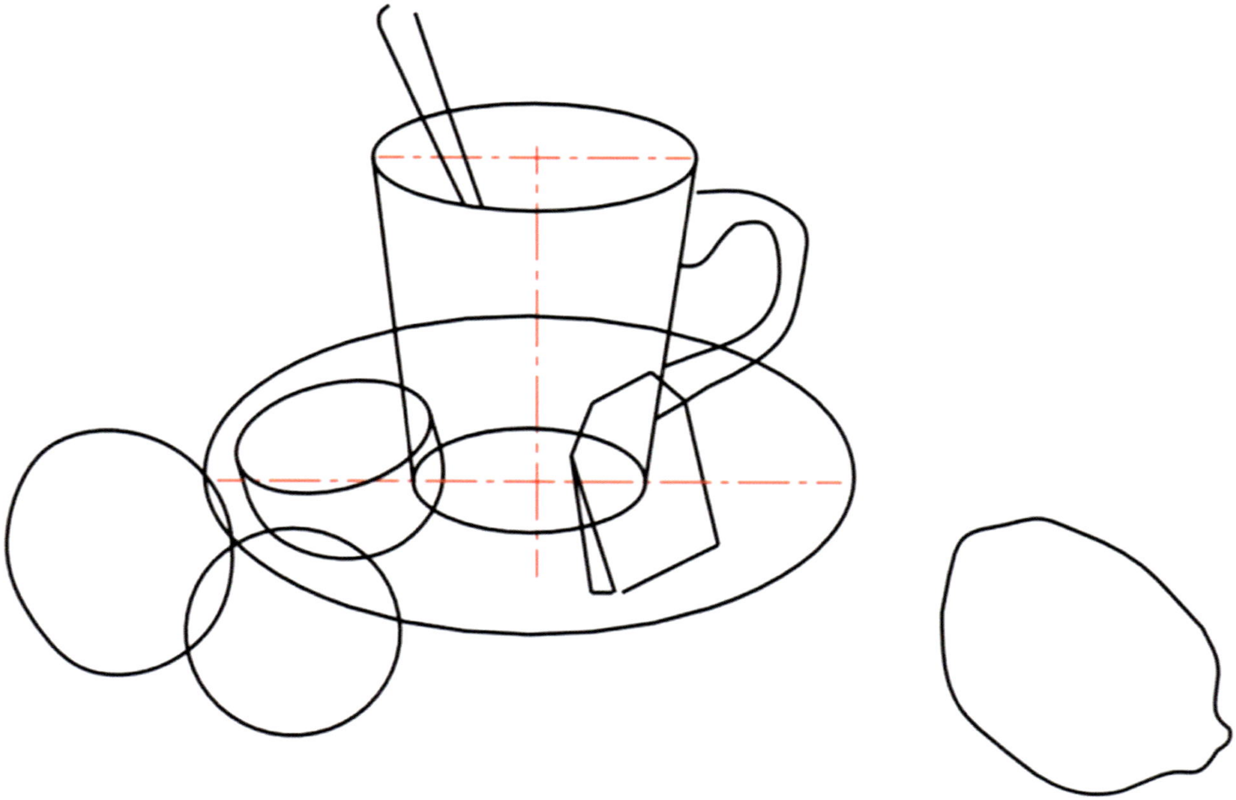

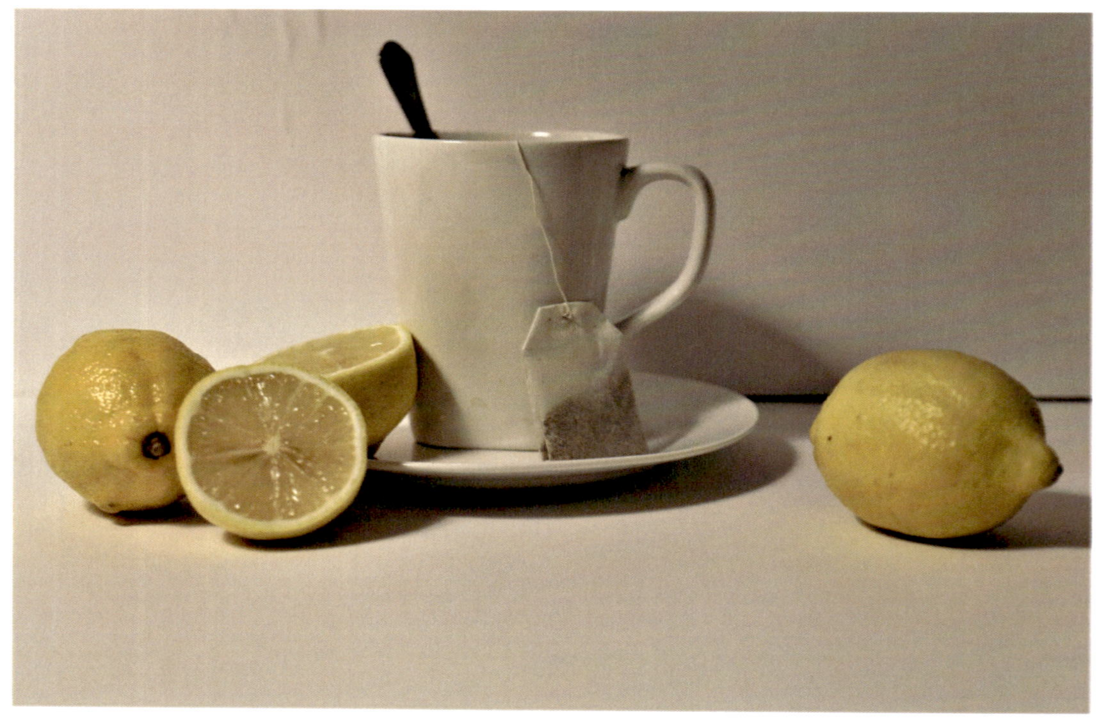

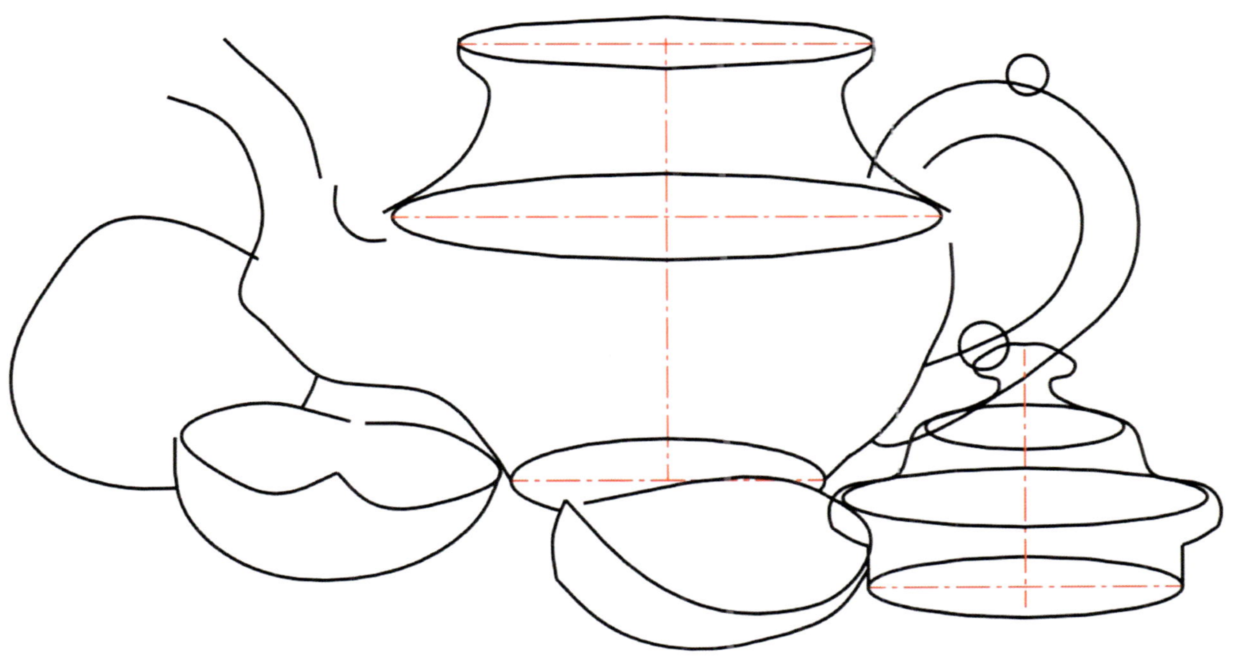

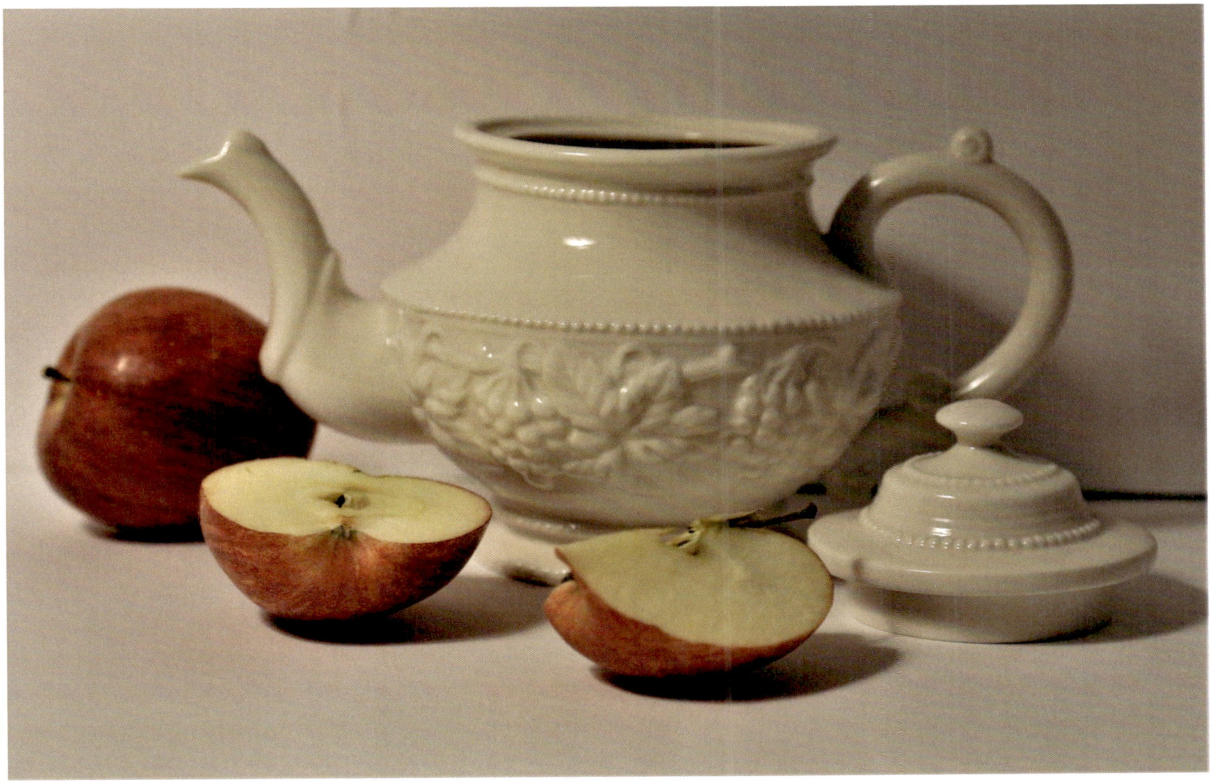

Introduction to Pastels - Focus Questions 2

Why are some things considered difficult to draw and other things considered easy to draw?

Most things are hard to draw because you may not have a wide range of reference and closeup details needed to understand the subject. Things that are easy to draw have simple shapes with clear details that we can interpret.

What do you think is hard to draw?

Things that we are unfamiliar with will be a challenge.

Do you think it is easier to draw from life, memory, or imagination? Why or why not?

As an artist, we have to be able to draw from life, memory, and imagination. Practice and seeing are the keys to drawing successfully with each.

What do you think of the Artist Daniel E. Greene?

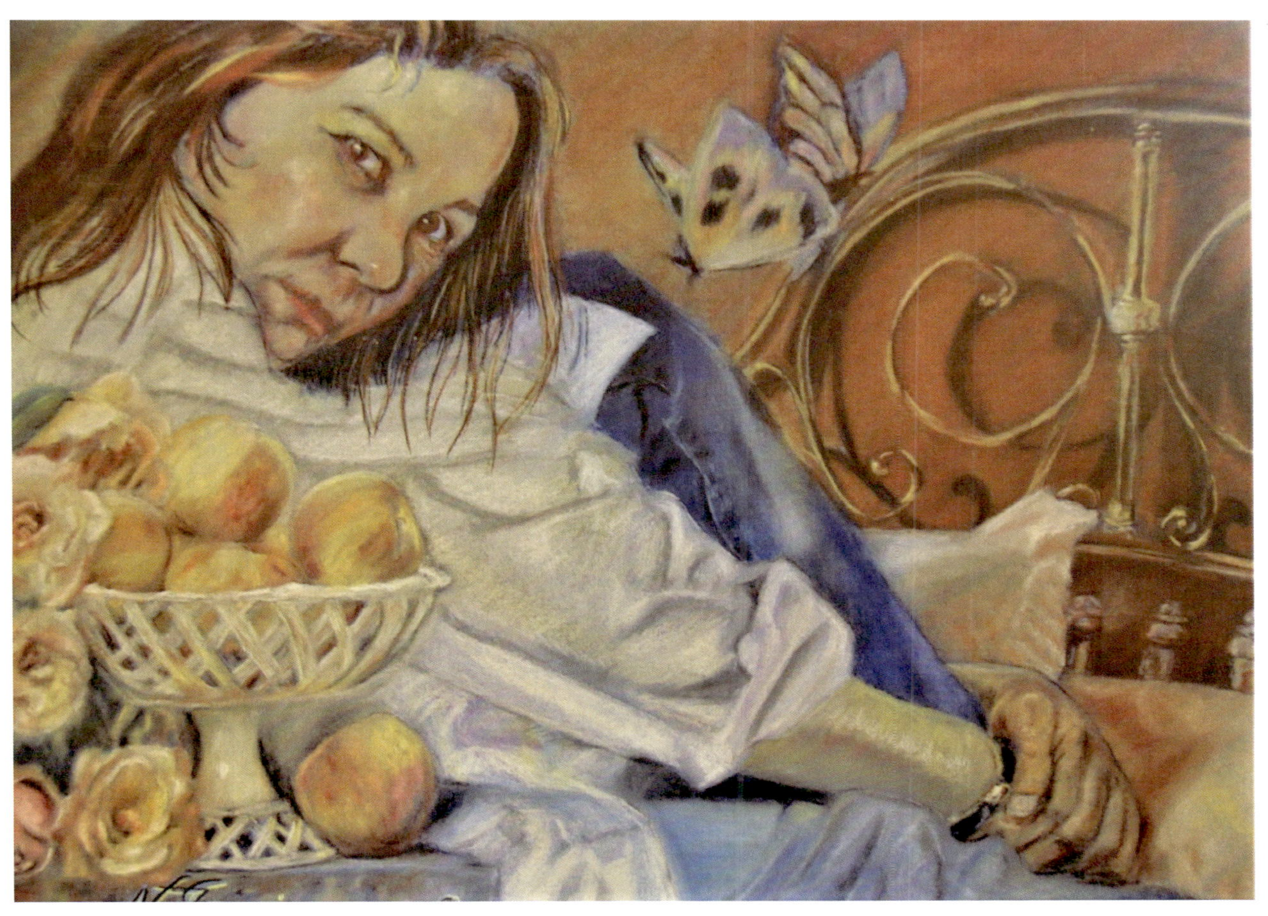

"Butterfly Dance" Pastel on pastel board, 2004

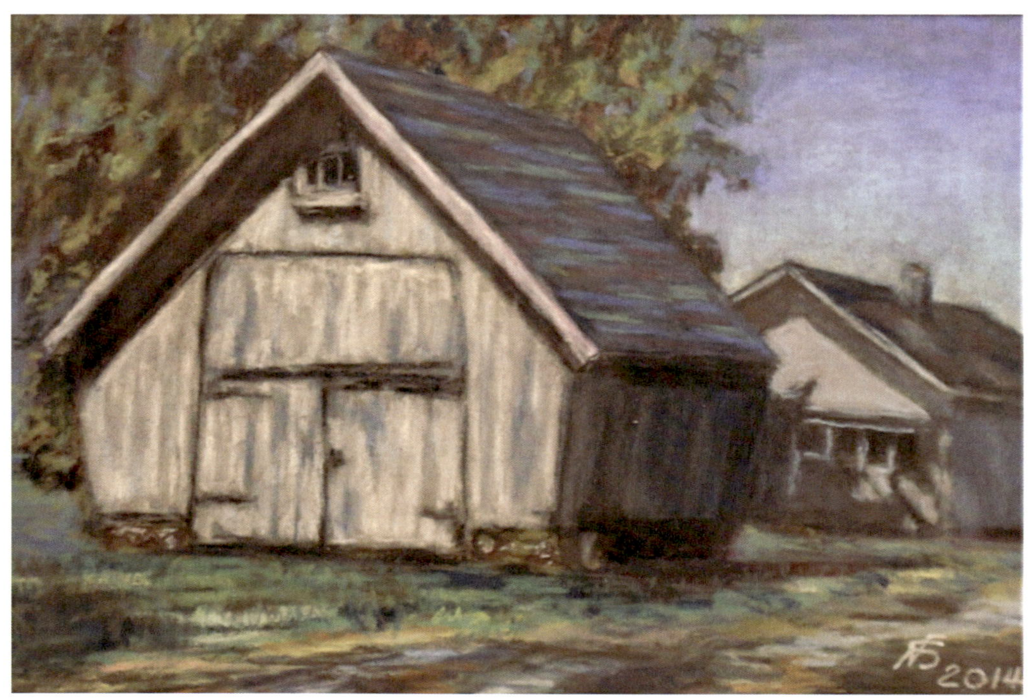

"Barns in Yardley" Pastel on pastel board, 2014

II. Working on Landscapes with Pastels

Pastels offer a great choice of colors and textures. Working with this medium will expand both the artist's drawing abilities and painting abilities. Let's start our landscapes artwork by getting some inspiration from the landscapes around us. Look for simple elements such as the sky, water, sand, and glass as the subject matter. Take several photos to use as your inspiration and reference.

Begin with a simple outline sketch, lightly drawing with a medium toned pastel, not too light or dark, on textured pastel paper. When choosing your paper, consider its tone or value rather than the paper's actual color. Gray or Tan is usually a good choice.

Next, Block in lightly the layer of color, creating the light shapes and dark shapes. You may want to experiment with different colors and strokes on a scrap sheet of paper throughout the process before applying the pastel on the main artwork surface. Avoid using white or black pastel in the early stages of your artwork.

Once the entire pastel area is filled in, begin blending the areas that you want to achieve a soft out of focus look. Try to avoid using your finger to blend with. Using a tortillon (Stump) would be preferred.

Finally, refine the artwork by adding more rich colors, and creating the illusion of distance by fading the background and adding irregular blades of thick and thin crisscrossing marks for grass in the foreground.

How Important is Abstract in Artwork?

All art is based on an artist applying some principles and elements of art to create his or her artwork. The artist will use various approaches and methods representing the artwork subject to be interpreted either realistically, abstractly or some of both. As the artist uses more abstraction (non-realism) in their artwork, the visual elements of art become more important. Beauty and taste become more in terms of the individual artist's style, and how the artwork is interpreted and evaluated.

As you develop as an artist, you may find yourself adding more abstract to your artwork to create a clearer message to the viewers. The artist may eliminate details and replace these areas with simpler abstract patterns and shapes. The more information the artist eliminates, the more abstract the art becomes. The artist may create various marks, textures, and strokes, creating more feeling and emotion within the artwork. These marks, textures, and strokes will induce an element of abstraction to the artwork that otherwise would not exist in reality.

Artists should understand abstraction; for it requires us to see clearly many possibilities when looking at our subjects. There are many abstract patterns in landscapes, rocks, foliage, trees, water, etc. Note: I am not telling you to be an abstract artist. I am telling you that putting emphasis on aesthetics (value, color, shape, etc.) within your artwork will make the artwork more abstract. As artists, you will have to not only look at a barn on the top of the hill, and see the barn, but also see the variations of values, lines, shapes, etc. within and around these shapes.

Demo Landscape 1

I begin this pastel landscape by selecting a main focal area or subject (a wave of water). I am working on a 11" x 14" pastel board. I place drafting tape around the inside for a 9-1/2" x 7-1/2" border opening, allowing spacing to place a Mat over the picture once it is completed. I drew this landscape using mostly my imagination, but the method of creating a layout with either charcoal or pastels is still my first step.

In this pastel painting, I worked on the focal areas and the background first. I then added the foreground by adding some warmer colors in the rocks. Finally, I added movement to the waves by showing the water crashing onto the rocks.

I give the artwork a name – " White Waves" and Sign and Date the work.

Note: In using pastel, it is easy to experiment with colors. I often use pastels to guide my color decisions before creating a painting in other mediums, such as oil or watercolor.

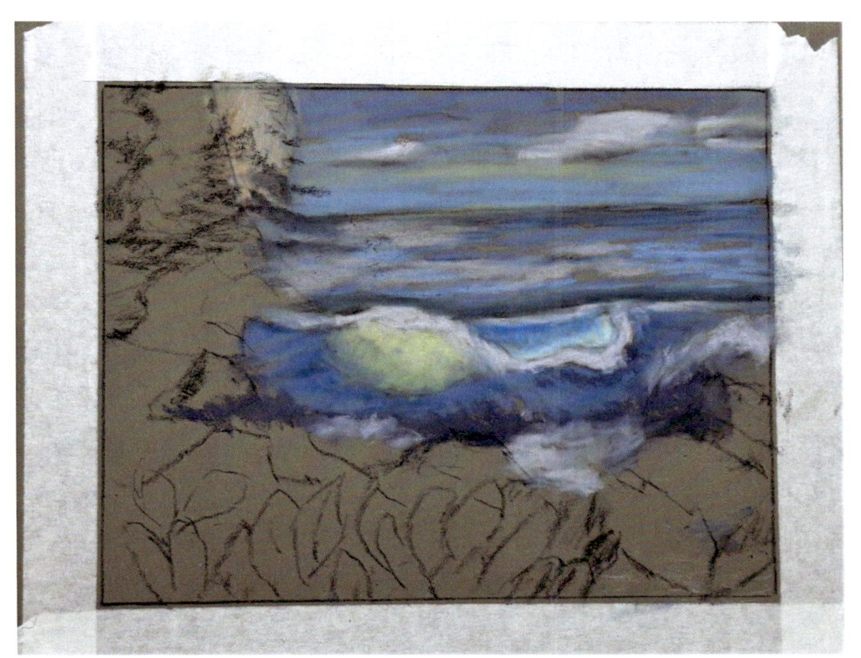

Working the Background Colors

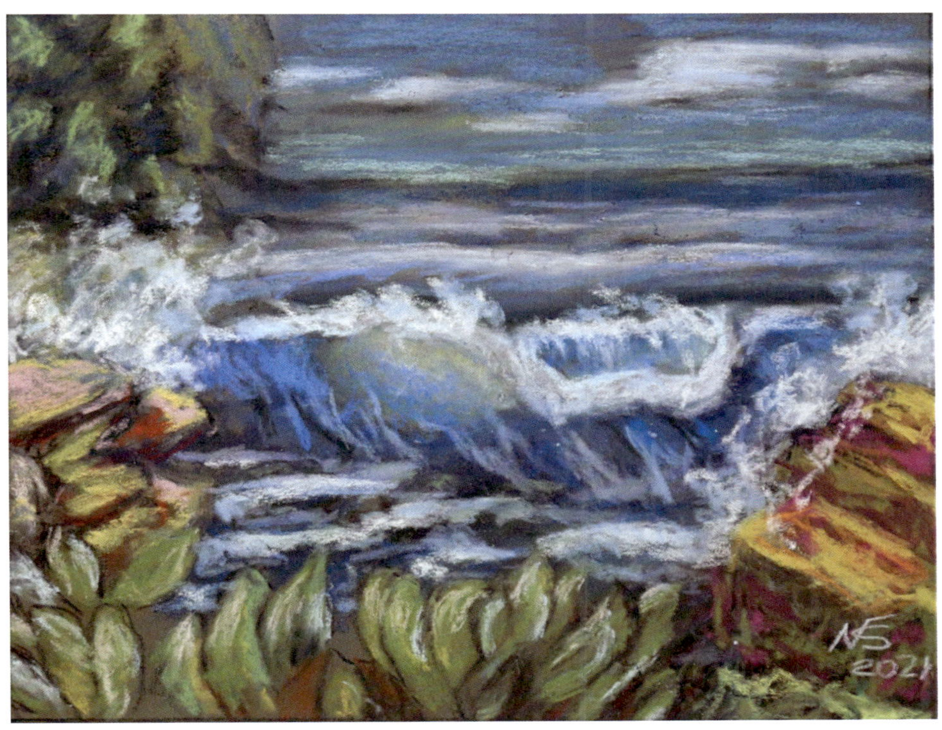

Add Emotion and Expression

Painting Landscape from Imagination

Creating imagined landscapes is like an artist being set free to interpret the world around him or her. Learning to draw from your imagination allows you to interpret wide open spaces filled with any number of subjects. This skill will help you develop and become a more creative artist.

The atmosphere of the artwork may be slightly or greatly different than the world around you. Feel free to separate the reality of the environments you see, and welcome the viewer to your imaginary world. The artist's landscapes, real or made-up, must be interesting and the elements within the painting must be balanced for both.

The artist, when painting real or imagined landscapes, has to decide what lighting effects and visual effects to apply, in order to engage viewers to the artwork they are viewing. Your worlds of art will be imaginary, but the inspiration that the artwork evokes from the color, space, wildlife, and other elements displayed will be pretty real to some viewers.

Artists explore and analyze subjects' imagery that inspire them, real or imagined, and from this, produce ideas of how to interpret this information visually. With a bit of imagination, artists reinterpret what they see or imagine and strive to create subjects in their own unique ways.

What to Do

You need a good imagination and an open mind.
On a piece of paper with charcoal and pastels, follow the steps below.

Step 1
Divide the paper with the sky and the land. The sky mass areas can be larger or smaller than the land mass areas, but do not make them equal in size.

Step 2
Use the charcoal sticks (point and sides) to fill in random marks for the sky and the land

areas. At this stage, do not try to draw subjects, such as clouds, trees, etc. Don't panic, for it may look a bit abstract at this stage.

Step 3

Use your pastels sticks to fill in random marks of colors for the sky and the land masses. Look at the marks you created and use your imagination to see the potential for creating landscape features from the random marks you have made. Are you able to see the cloud shapes, or distant hills? If you are having trouble, take a break and come back later and look at the abstract shapes again.

Step 4

Once you have established some sort of balanced composition, create an illusion of depth in your landscape by using paler tones in the background and darker, more colorful tones, in the foreground.

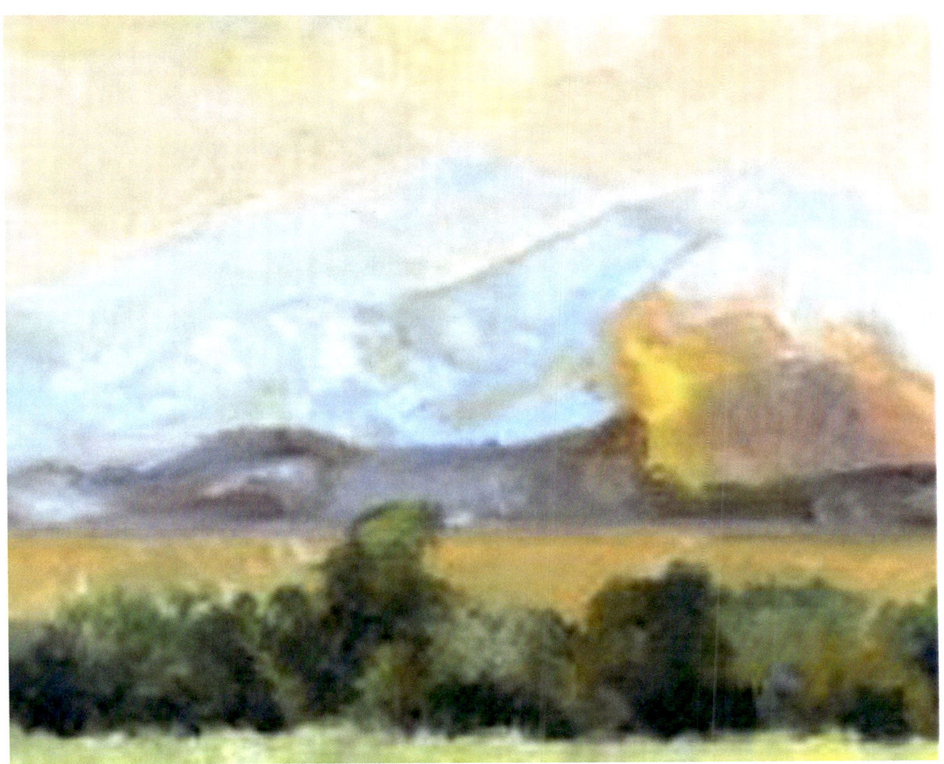

Creating Landscape from Imagination

Assignment: BK 5-02 Landscapes

Use at least one of the reference landscape paintings to draw and add color using pastels. You may change these paintings or use your own landscape reference photos and imagination.

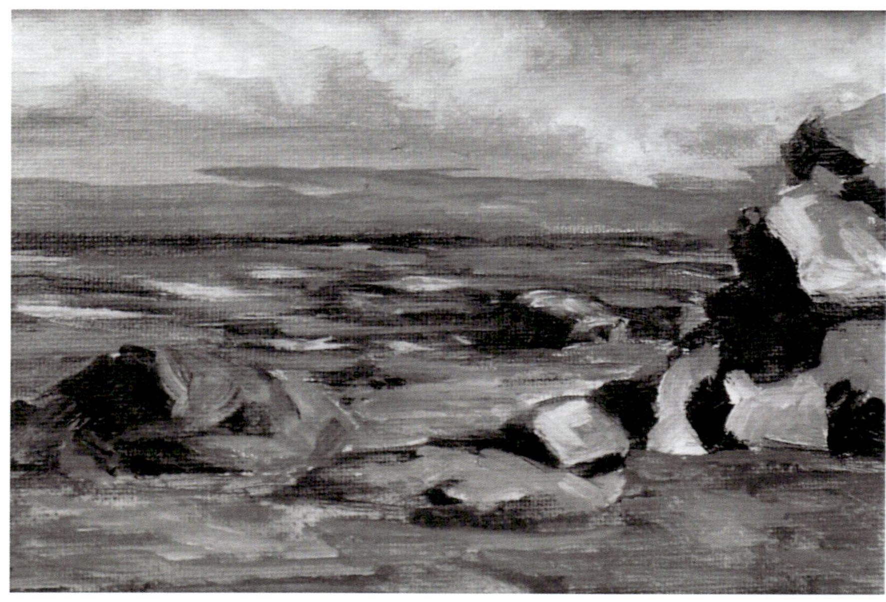

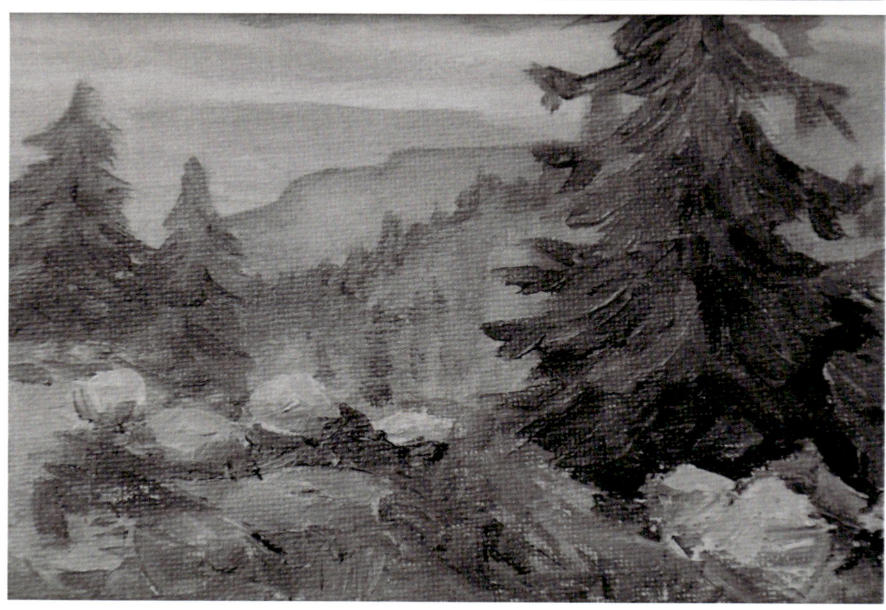

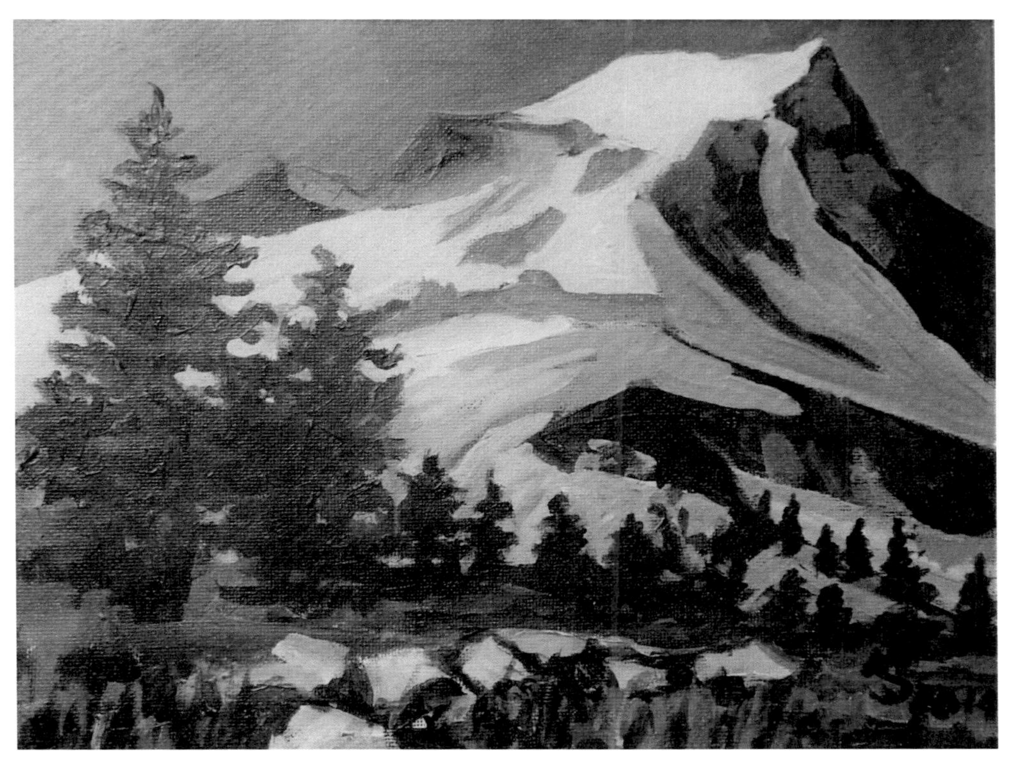

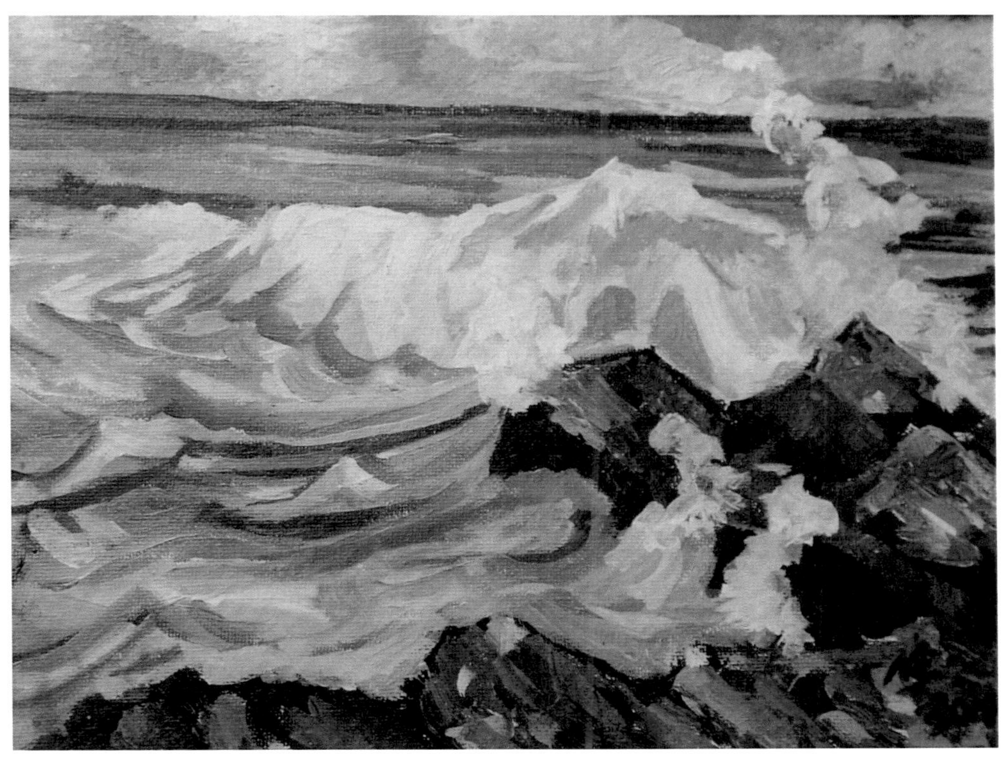

III. Working with Portraitures and Animals

The History Behind Portraits

Once upon a time, portraiture was reserved to those who had the means to commission such tributes - only the rich and the influential could be immortalized by having their images survive beyond their lifetime.

Now it is open to all. We can all outlive ourselves, having portraits done without being of high social backgrounds. Portraiture painting is not only for the special persons who have influenced others and who have accomplished great tasks during their lifetimes. For the artist, portraiture is for understanding and discovering the human spirit. Still, it is the artist's responsibility to transfer and manipulate the image and character of the subject and place it onto the canvas to show the subject's character in his or her true light.

Portraiture has been with us for at least 5,000 years - Egyptians excelled at it, as did the Romans. Nothing tells us about the human condition quite as effectively as portraiture. In the portraiture, everything tends to pivot about the face. The face is the place toward which the eye naturally navigates in order to understand the full nature of what this person stands for and represents. We can visually see the person feeling happy, sad, angry, and so on by examining the person's gestures.

Photography Versus Painting

Photography will produce hyperrealism in a photo; thus, this should not happen in a painting. A painter is not trying to compete with photography. Although a painter can with painstaking accuracy produce a replica of a photo-realistic painting on canvas, doing this is like unedited realities where the viewer may be amazed at the details, but miss the message that he or she has to seek out for his or her own self.

The face is what the artist is trying to depict in a very particular way, showing the personality of the person in his or her clothes surrounded by a meaningful background that is inseparable from the subject's uniqueness. The artist is telling this person's story and should highlight who this person is. Composing a portrait is more than a question of how true the likeness is to the person. Size, scale, shape, and viewpoint are all important aspects for any fine art painting; portraiture is no different.

Working from Photographs in Drawing the Portrait

Artists working from photographs need to understand that in order to create realistic forms, they must have an indication of a light source. Before you can define the features on the human face, you much first define the skull to place the human face on.

Value, not color, will create this illusion. If you are using a camera that has a flash, you will have to turn your flash off, for it will decrease the amount of shadow and light contrasting on the face. This will make it harder for artists to understand the true structure and form of the head. Seeing the shadows and lights also will aid in proportionally placing the features in the correct location. Look at how adding the lights and shadows aid the representation of the head shown here.

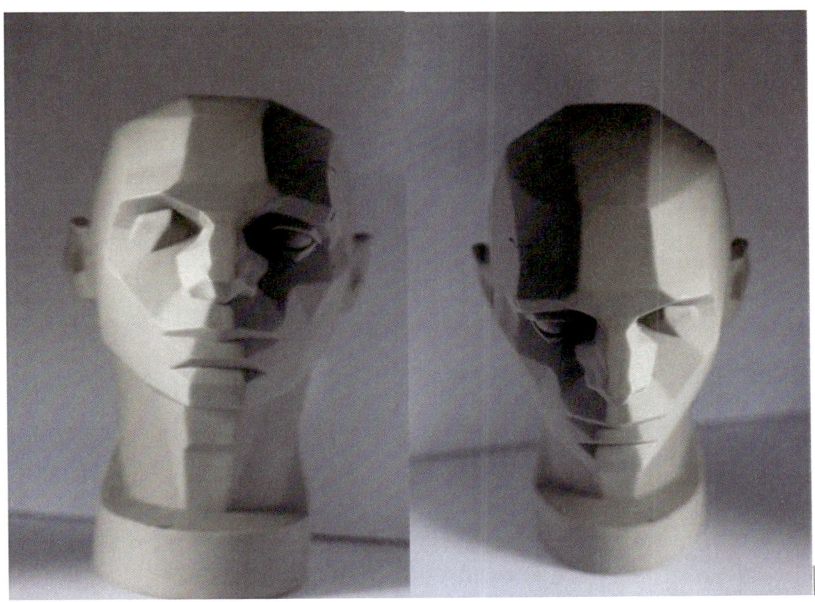

Head with light and shadow shown on planes of the Face.

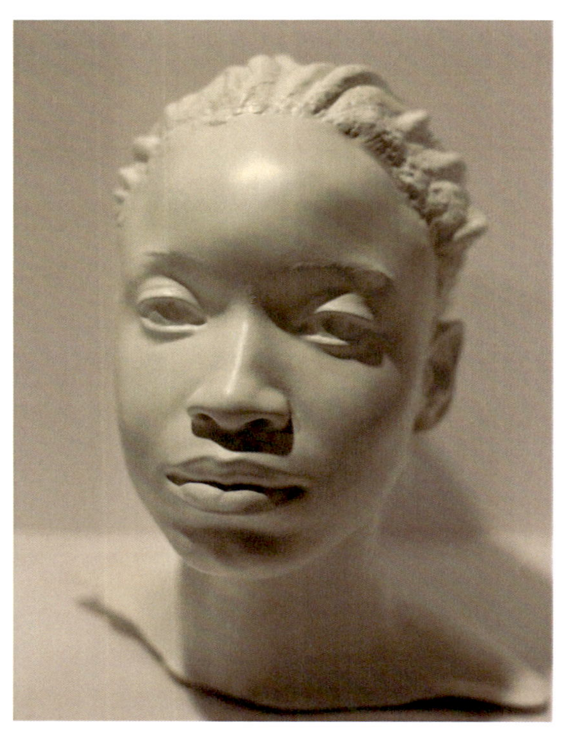

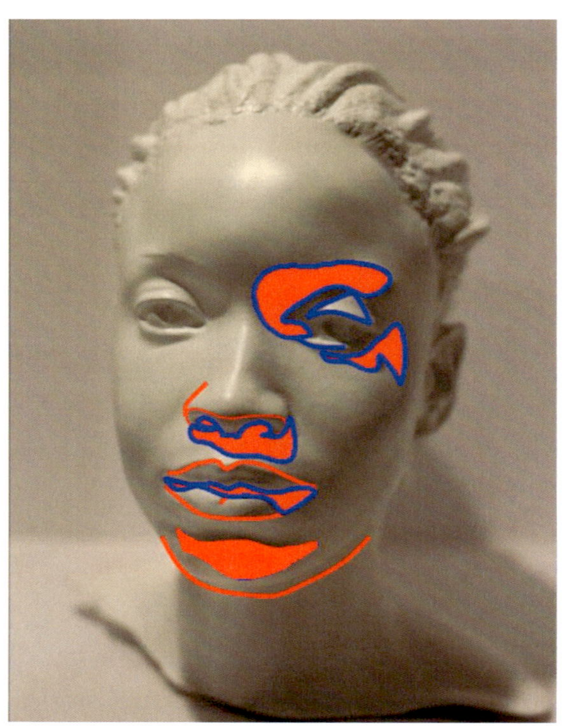

Looking for the abstract shapes (lights and darks) to create a portrait likeness.

The Abstract Shapes Create the Form and Likeness

Before adding the features of the face (eyes, noses, lips, etc.), the artist should take a closer look at the abstract shapes that are created by the light hitting the face structure. Defining these abstract shapes of lights and darks will create the subject likeness. This technique of using chiaroscuro (Italian for chiaro, "light" and Scuro, "dark") was used by Leonardo da Vinci and others artists in the 15 century.

Above, on the right, I highlighted some of the woman's casted shadows shapes in red. Being able to clearly see casted shadows, form shadows, reflective lights, and highlights shapes will give the artist the ability to create 3-dimensional illusions.

Planning: The 3 S's in Portraiture

In considering the **size, shape, and space** of a portrait painting, a head-and-shoulders portrait looks nice in a "portrait format" where the shape is taller than it is wide. Large portraits create an impact by their sheer size alone and suggest the subject is prominent in society or wealthy. The larger the image, the more expensive the material, and the longer it takes the artist to complete the work. Small portraits tend to be more personal and intimate.

Still, the artist has to decide how much of the subject to include:

The head, shoulders, and upper chest.
Half length - common in seated poses.
Full length - proclaiming a person's grandeur and superiority.

Psychologically, we focus our attention first on the human face and its features; therefore, moving further out in the portrait painting will give the artist an opportunity to suggest more about the subject's interests and situation in life.

Sometimes what is left out of a portrait painting may say more about the subject than what is left in. The viewer is invited to imagine life beyond the confines of the canvas. Cropping and deliberately truncating a subject may imply many things -- Was the subject moving? Was the subject not posing at all?

Multiple Portraits Paintings

The artist is challenged when he or she is depicting more than one person in a portrait. The overall relationships have to be suggested in how the group is posed, as well as the relationships through the composition. The artist must arrange spaces to suggest isolation by contrasting positive forms with empty negative space. These gaps between positive forms will strengthen the composition and make the painting more interesting with the suggestion of depth.

In conclusion, I would like to say that you really need to understand and know the people you are creating a portrait for. Make many sketches and studies of several possibilities before beginning the work. Make it personal.

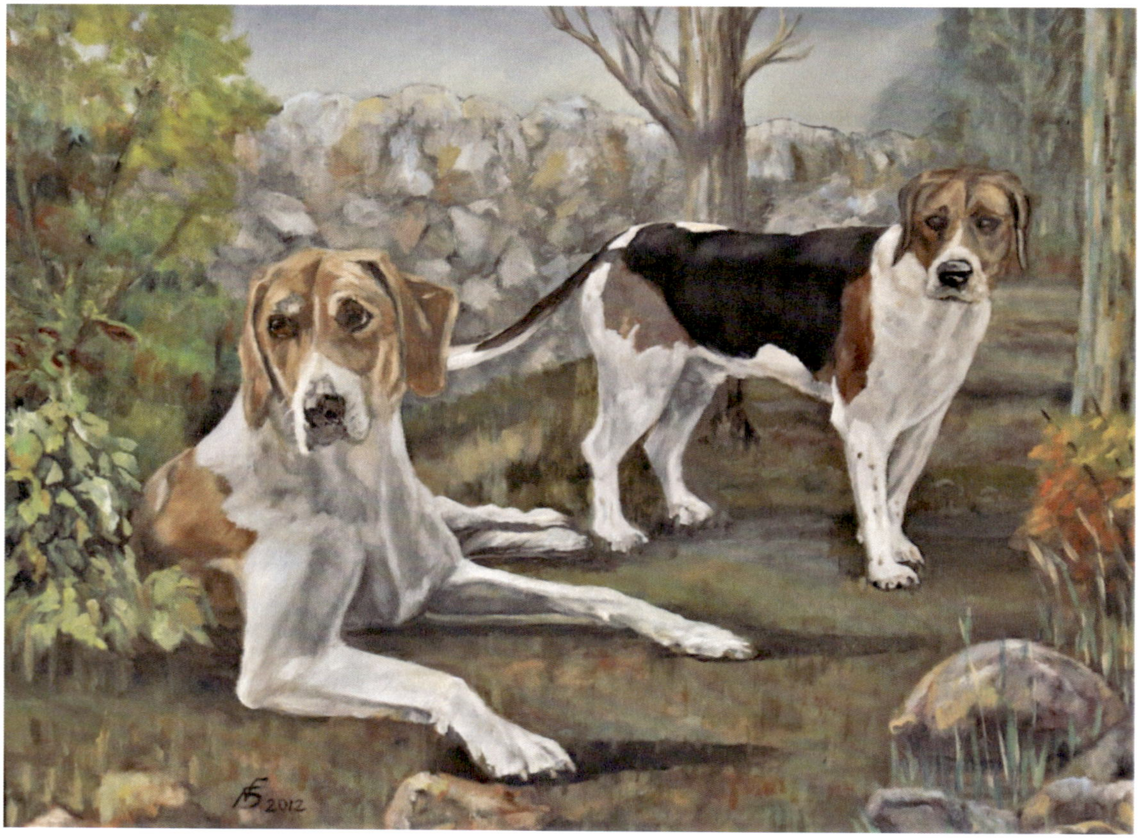

"Jess and Louie" Oil on linen, 2012

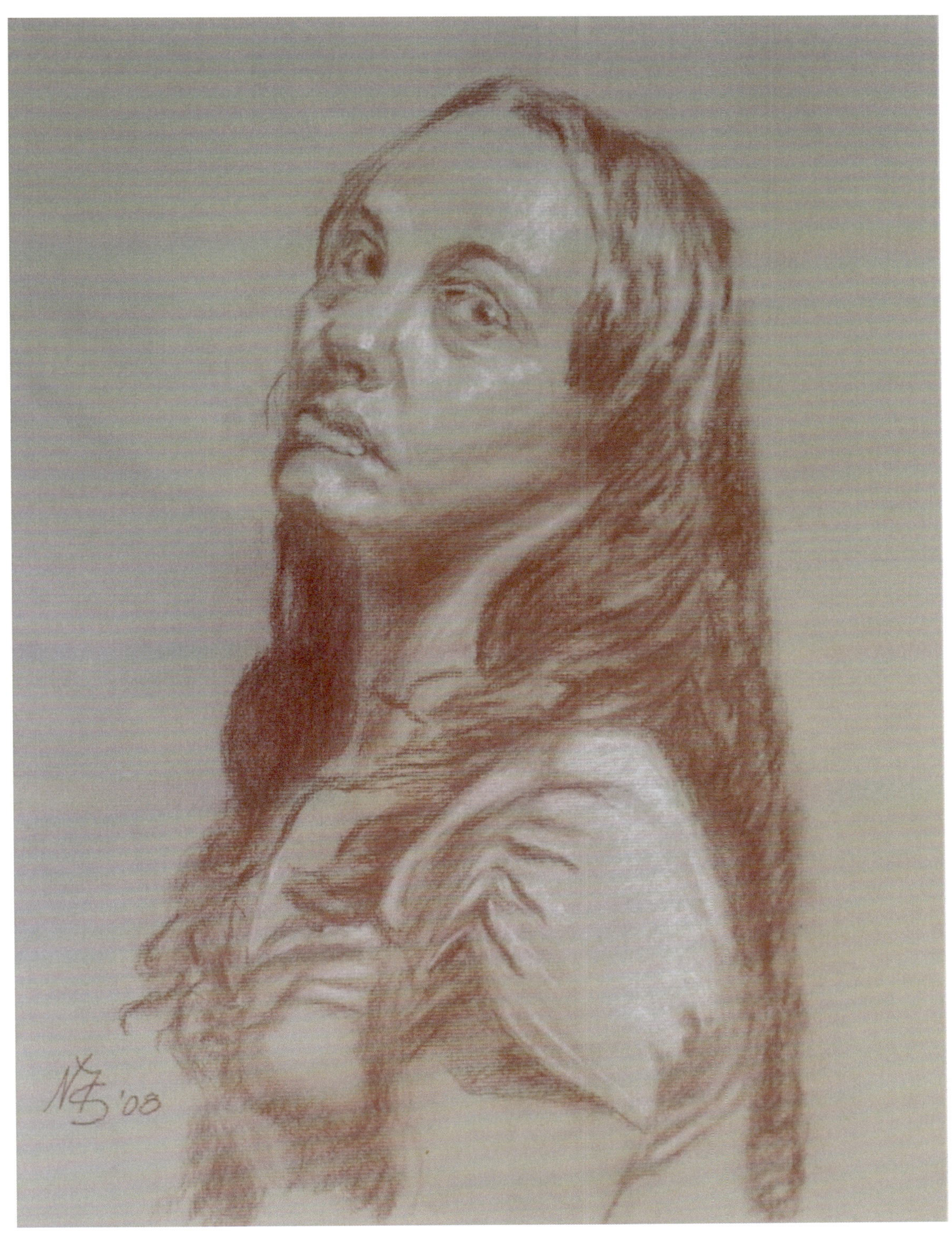

"Female Study" Pastel on toned paper, 2008

Seeing the Emotions of Colors

Colors are described abstractly, usually referring to temperature (cold, cool, warm, or hot) or by tint and shade (light, pale, dark, or bright). Phrases, such as "I am feeling blue," "I am green with envy," or "You're yellow," relate colors to feelings. Color is a vibration of light; it affects not only our eyes but also our whole body, so it has become one of the important elements that must be understood by the serious artist. After reading many books on color, here is what I have discovered about color. I will attempt to unravel a small part of this complex mystery in the following paragraphs.

What we do know about color is that hot colors are strong and aggressive and affect people by increasing blood pressure and stimulating the nervous system. Cold colors are dominating and strong and slow down the metabolism and increase one's sense of calm. Warm colors are comforting, spontaneous, and welcoming. Cool colors are soothing, calm, and comforting. Light colors are relaxing and suggest airiness, rest, and liquidity. Dark colors are concentrated and serious. Pale colors (containing about sixty-five percent white) are soft and romantic. Bright colors (with the omission of gray or black) attract attention, and are exhilarating and cheerful.

Color is an important aspect of an image, and as an artist, he or she must understand this impact in order to communicate to viewers. It evokes the audience's emotions and gets them involved within the piece. When thinking about the different emotions, the artist needs to select the correct color combination to bring forth the desired mood.

The best way to understand color is to look around you and experience the red roses and their bright green leaves or the dark browns and grays in an old military office. Write down how you feel at that moment. You will always be correct in your observation.

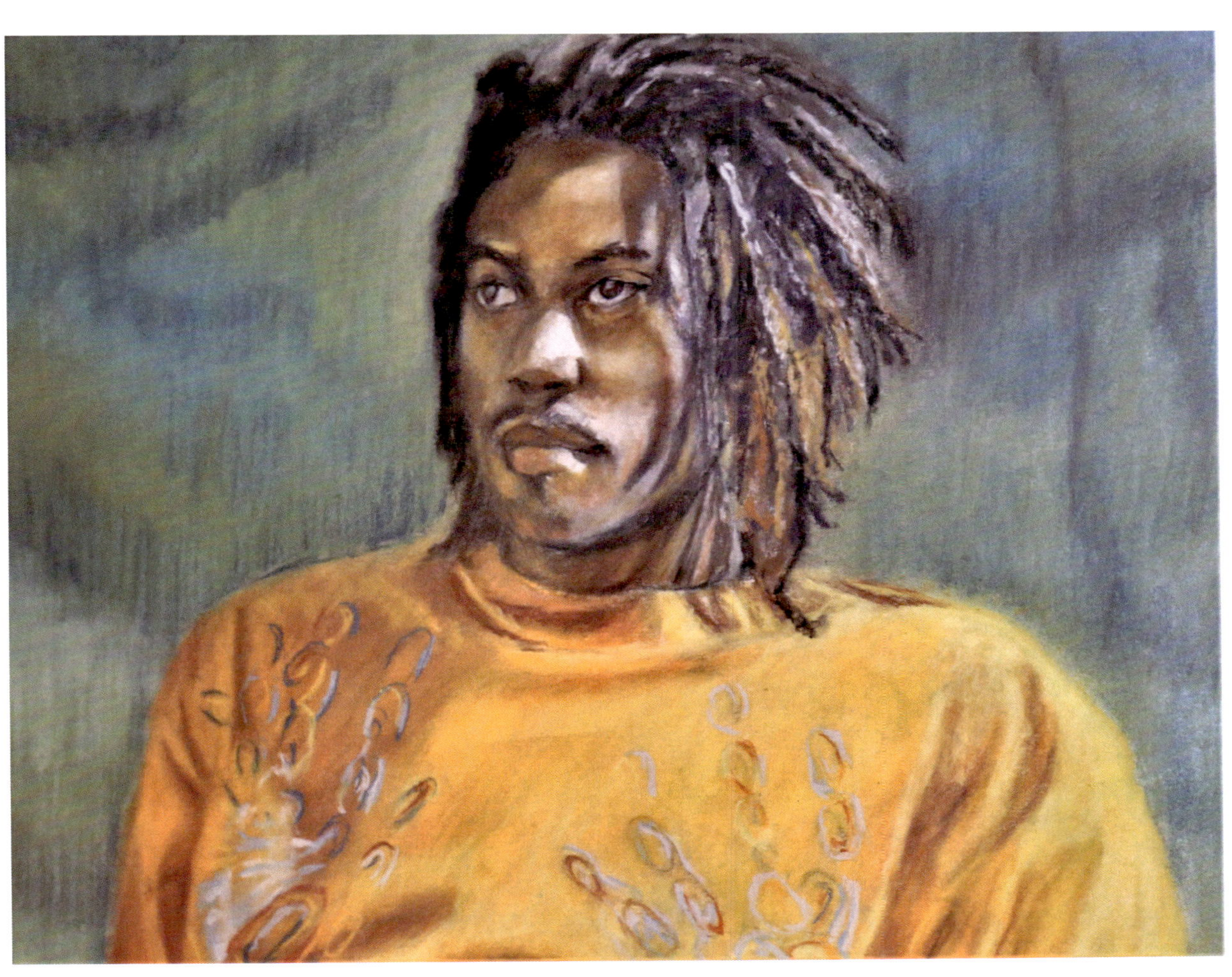

"The Artist Son" Pastel on toned paper, 2012

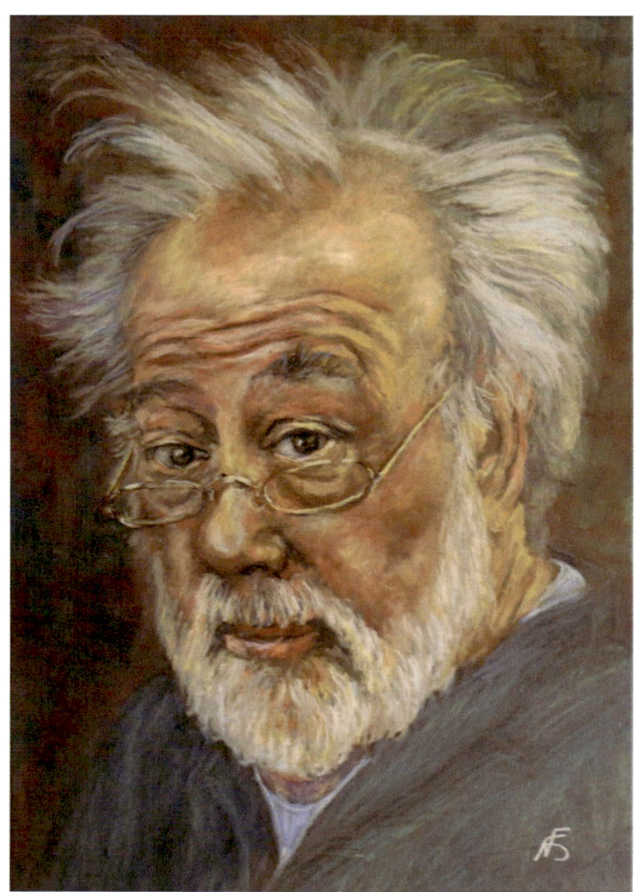

Upper Left: ***"Picture Framer" Pastel on toned board, 2014***

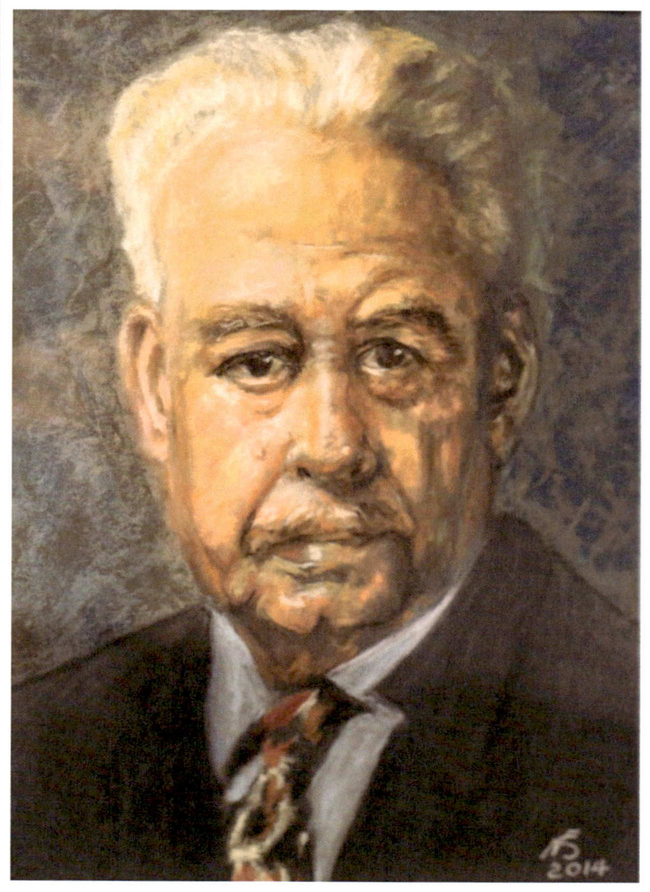

Lower Right: ***"Boss Man" Pastel on toned board, 2014***

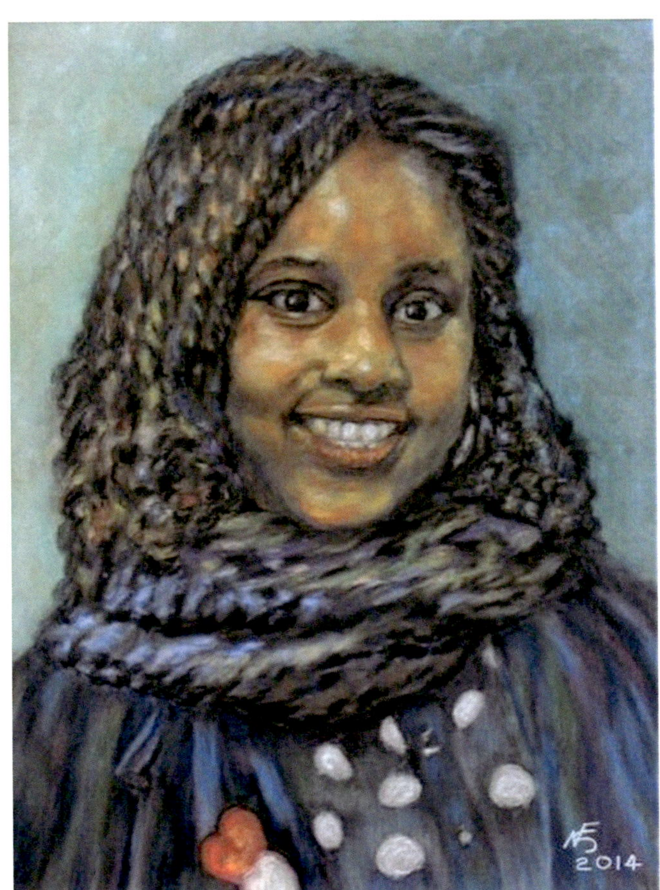

Upper Left: ***"Valentine" Pastel on toned board, 2014***

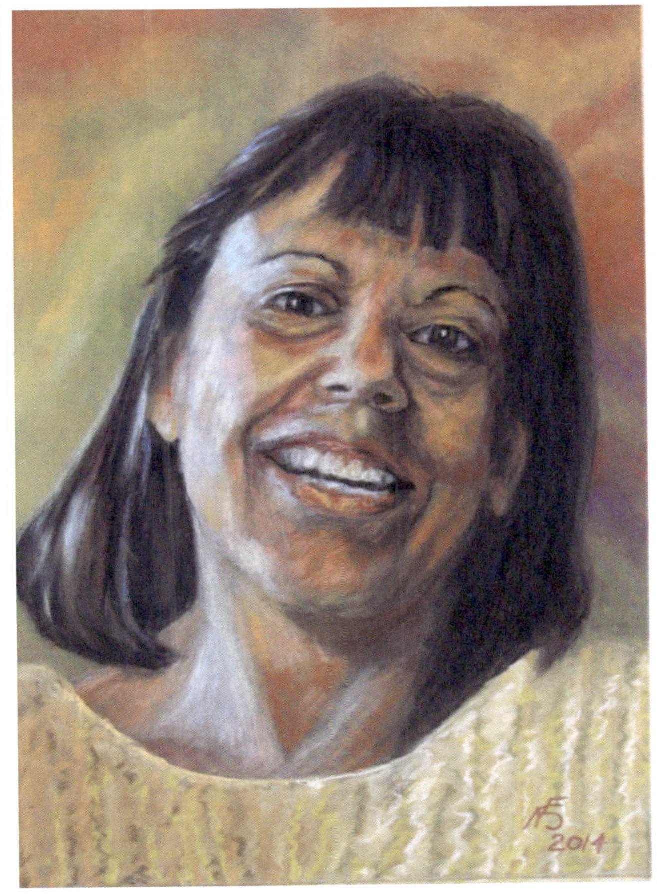

Lower Right: ***"Sun Rays" Pastel on toned board, 2014***

How to Set Up for Portraits?

There are three elements that need to be addressed in creating a successful portrait. These three elements are the pose, the clothing, and the environment. The pose is by far the most important for it will determine the message that is delivered to the viewer. Clothing will reveal social status, age, and period of time of the moment. The environment for formal portraits is usually set somewhere within the corporations, universities, or organizations that the subject is representing, whereas the environment for informal portraits will portray the individuality of the subject.

The Pose: The pose is the facial expression, formal or informal. These characteristics are determined by looking at how relaxed the pose is. Are the hands casual or carefree? Is the pose candid? There are endless amounts of gestures and moods that will suggest who the portrait represents. The more the artist knows his model, the truer the personality will be represented.

The Clothing: The clothing should not overpower the attention to the face. For the formal male portraits, traditionally darker clothing has been used. For the formal female portraits, lighter clothing is fine to be used as it gives the portrait a sense of freshness. The clothing in informal portraits describes an attitude or occupation and may include sunglasses, uniforms, jeans, and an endless number of possibilities to enable and enhance the personality of the viewer.

Environments: A formal portrait will usually be in a dark-muted color and will be set up in a subdued office setting. An informal portrait will be in a location that most reflects what the subject loves and that contributes to the individuality of the subject, such as walking along a beach, at a bus stop, or any number of places that best represent the subject's joys or lifestyles.

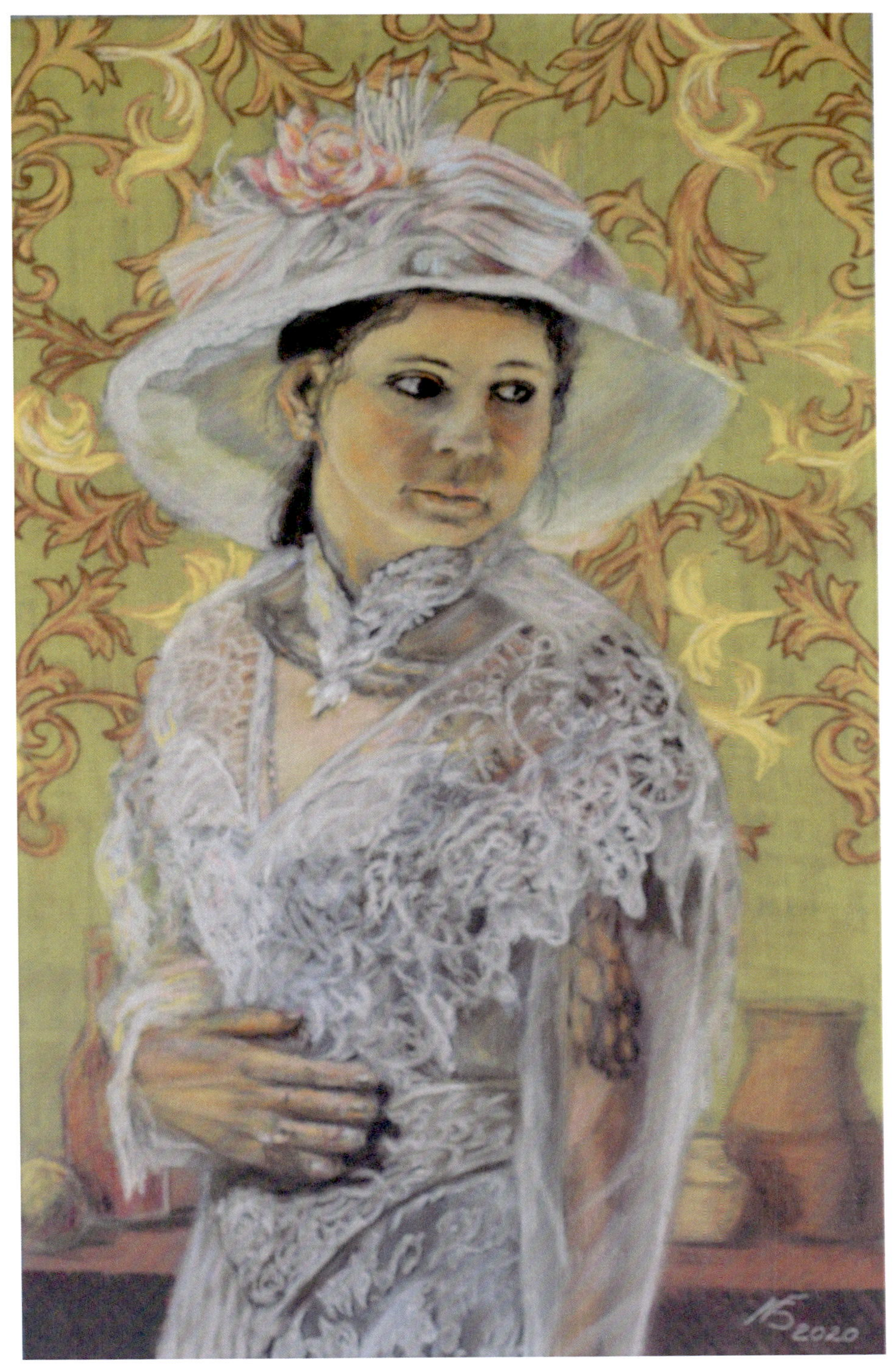

"Victoria" Pastel on pastel board, 2020

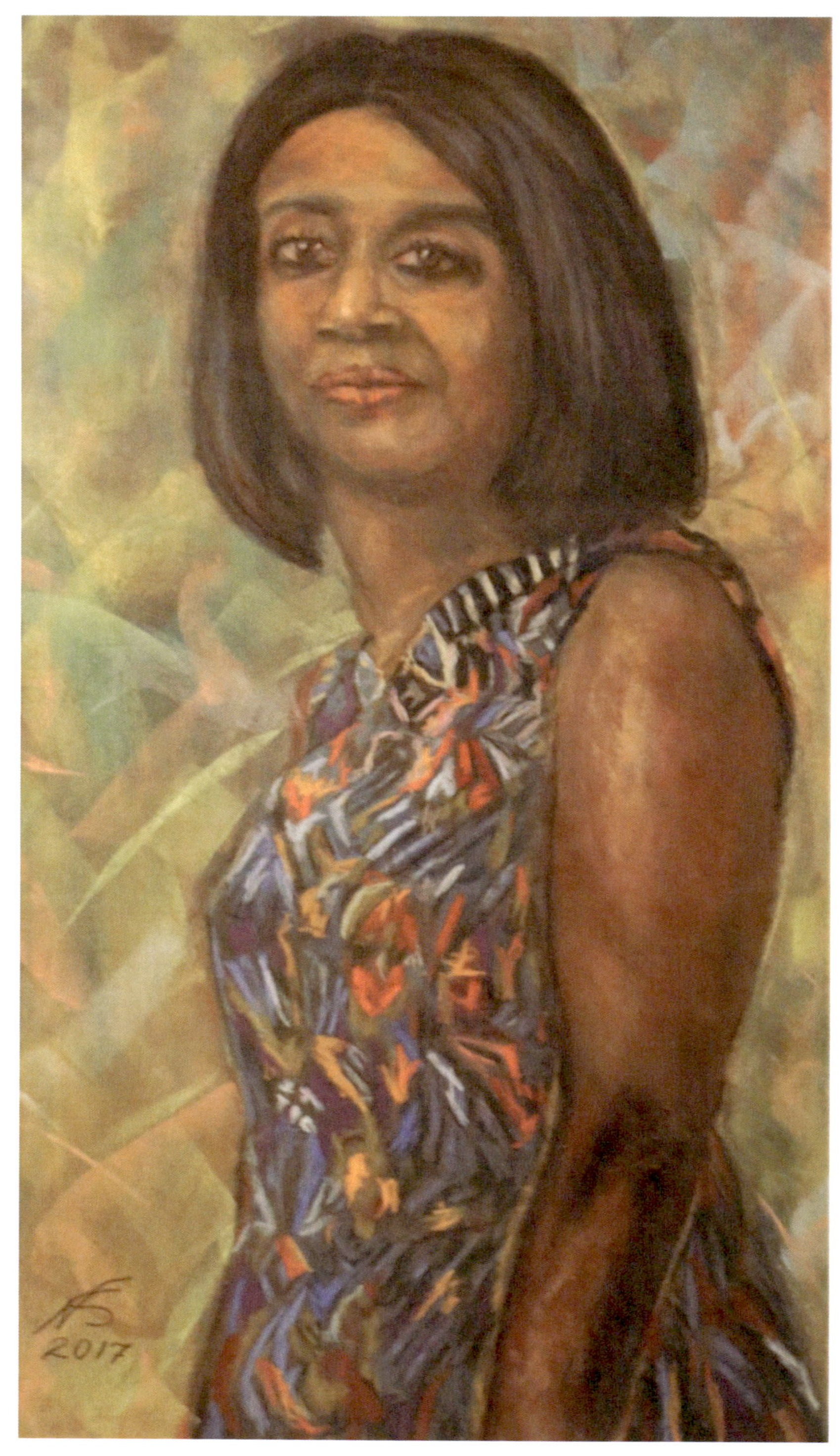

"Philly Girl" Pastel on pastel board, 2017

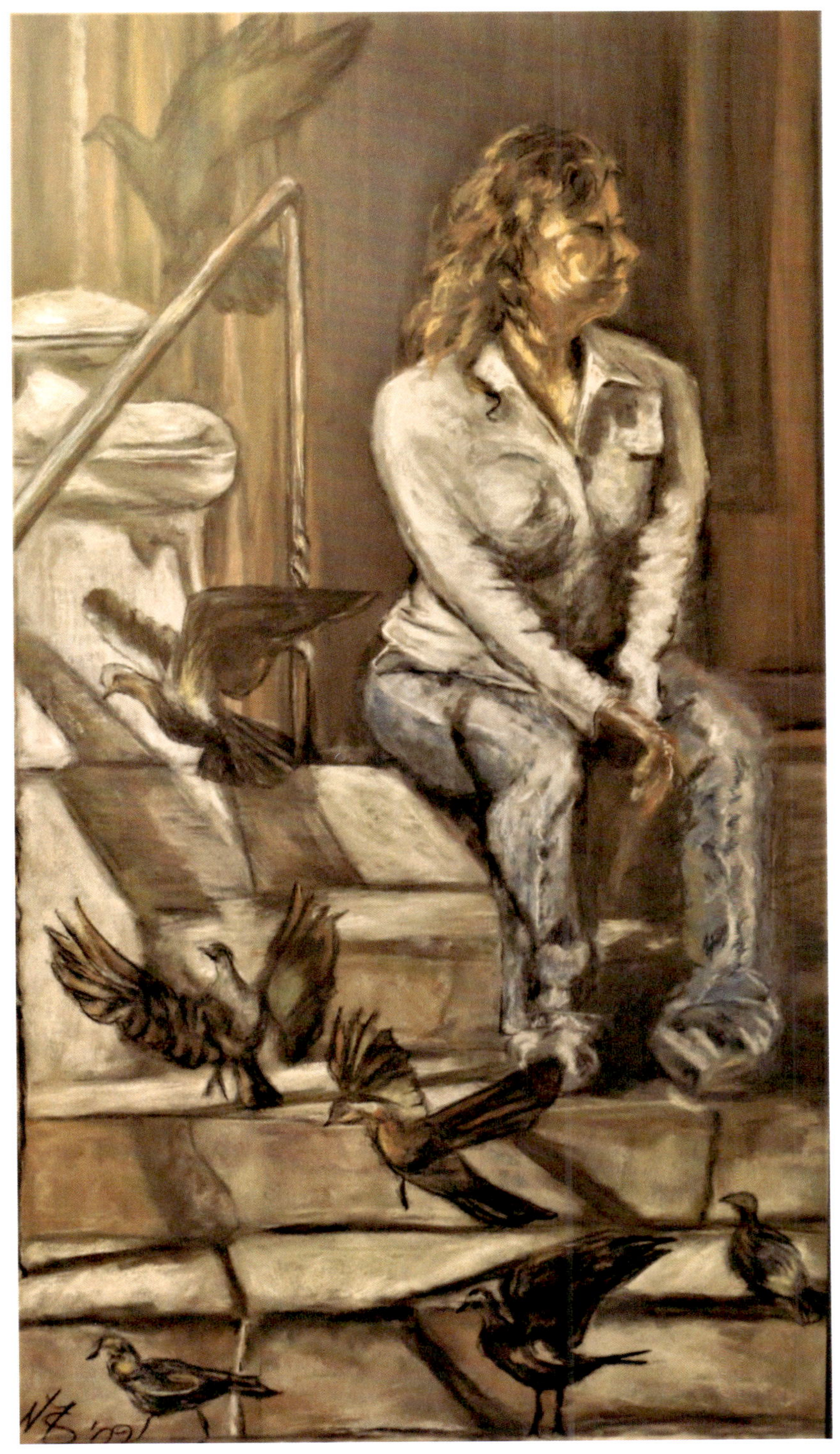

"Church Steps" Pastel on pastel board, 2009

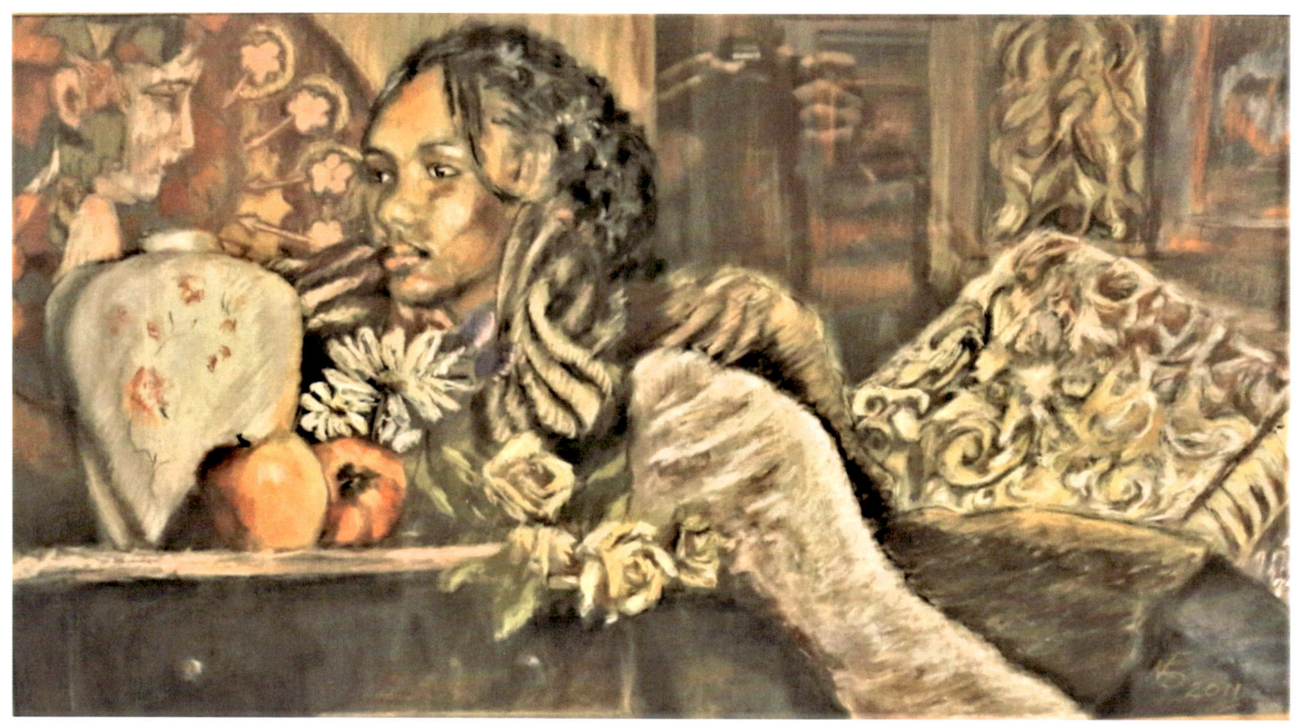

"Queen Randi" Pastel on toned board, 2011

Adding Expression to your Artworks

Now that you can draw, how do you express your artwork more creatively? How do you show the passion of what you have created or want to create in a more exciting and interesting way? In art, many artists will indirectly become illustrators telling a story.

An example of an Artist who told great stories within his artworks was Norman Rockwell, who for many years created over 300 illustrated (painting) covers for *The Sunday Evening Post*.

As an artist, you will decide on the individual mood (how expressive should the poses be). This may require you to adjust the facial features, clothing, and surrounding items to create a clearer story. In your artwork, is it clear who your character is or who he or she represents -- a doctor, a teacher, a president or whatever? How is the character interacting with the other elements within the artwork? Are the various items and individual or individuals in harmony with each other?

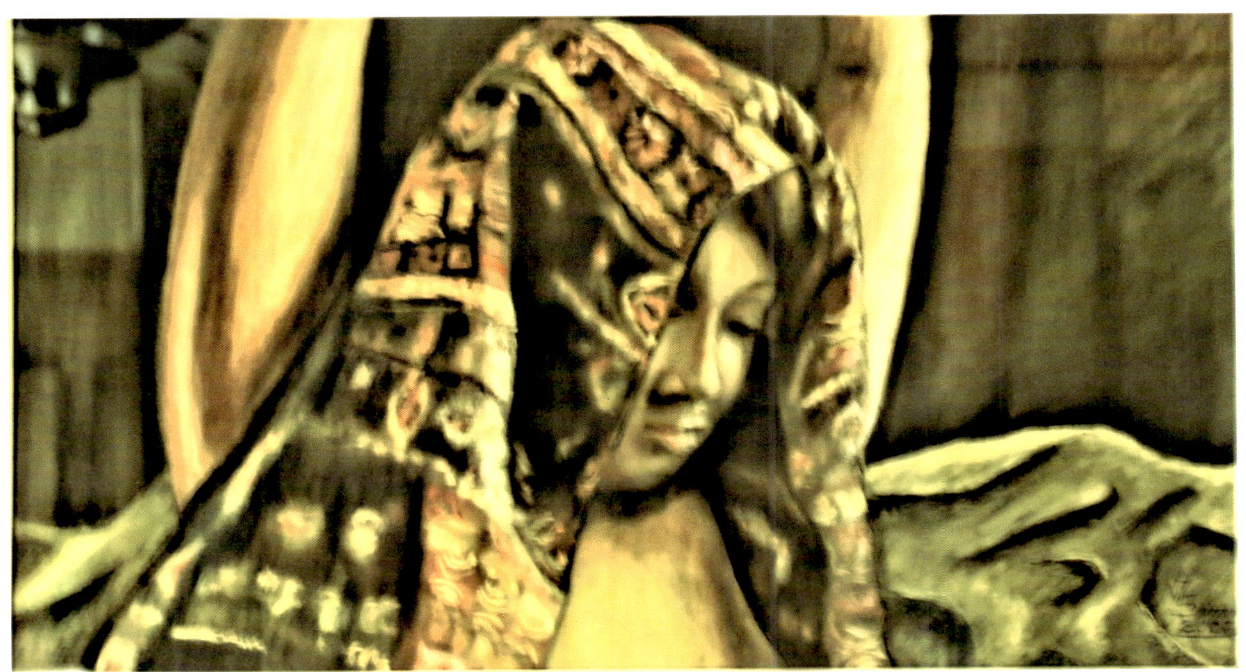

"Surrender" Pastel on toned board. 2007

Spend more time on the focal points (your subject) adding details before planning for other elements. Add expression to your subjects' facial features, their poses and movements, and interactions with their environment. Illustrating emotion can be conveyed with facial expression, but also with colors. Understanding color theory is in book six in this series, which will discuss how to understand what various colors and color palettes' moods they will convey.

Why Create Nude Art?

In both the works of past artists [such as the French artist Pierre-Paul Prud'hon (1758-1823) or the Italian artist Michelangelo di Lodovico Buonarrorti Simoni (1475-1564)] and the present master artists of the twenty-first century [such as Anthony (Tony) Ryder or Costa Vavagiakis and many others], the nude figure is still very much admired. But we are at an age where many do not consider the importance of the nude figure and consider it inappropriate as fine art to be hung in their homes.

The reason for this is due to the masses' inability to see beyond the implied negative sexuality of nude figures and the inability to separate the representation of ideal arrangements of beautiful forms from the massive pornography and sexual images that are distributed on the Internet and in publications and advertisements.

Still, drawing and painting the nude figure is one of the best ways to increase your creativity and drawing ability. This is because the human body, although it has its proportions, is also alive, and to recreate this vitality, the artist cannot simply reproduce the human form's gestures and spirit as he or she would create a still life artwork.

The nude figure is foremost a beautiful work of art within itself, and it is a challenge for the artist to create a divine work of art full of energy, passion, and a host of other wonderful moods within his drawing or painting.

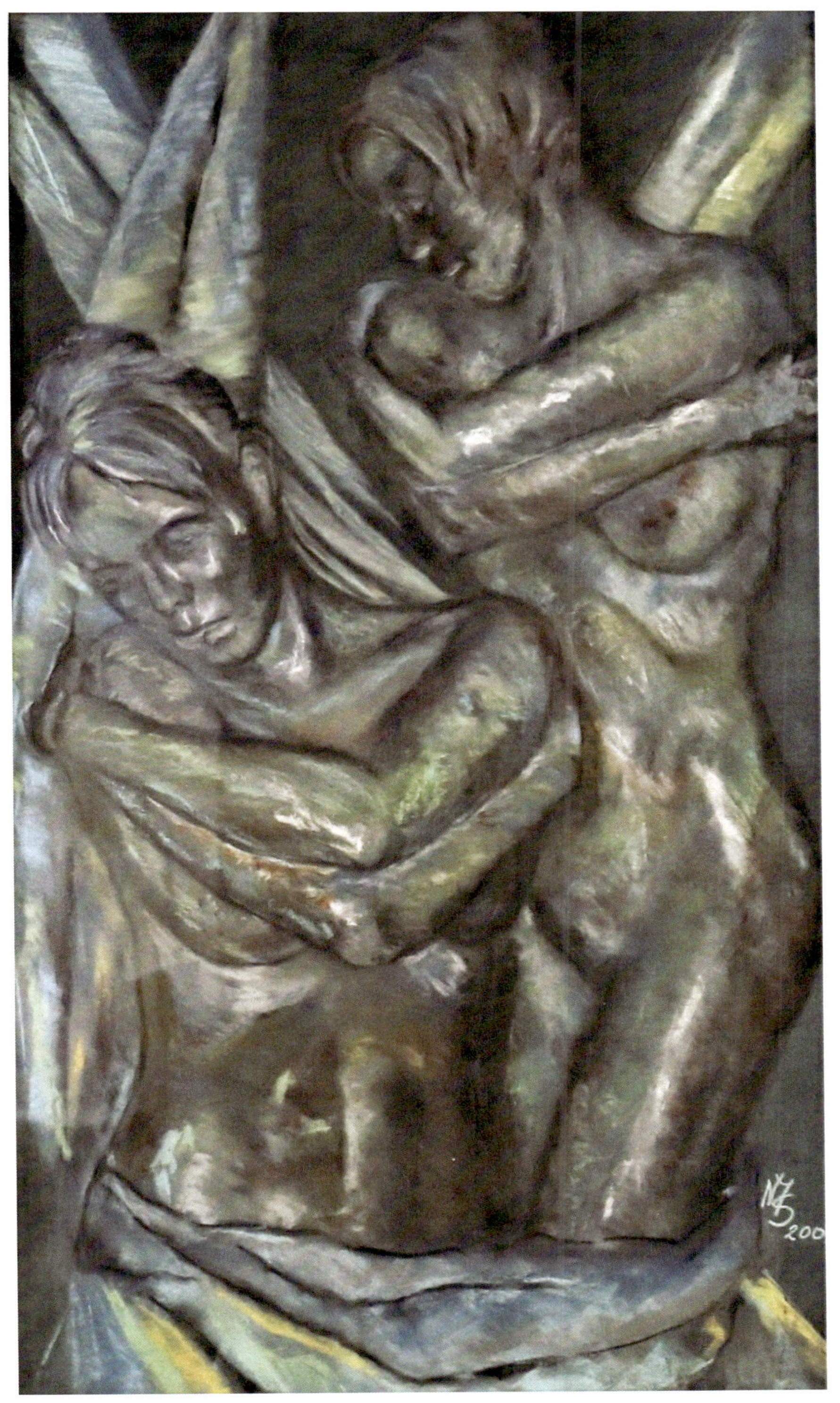

"Bronze Statues" Pastel on pastel board, 2007

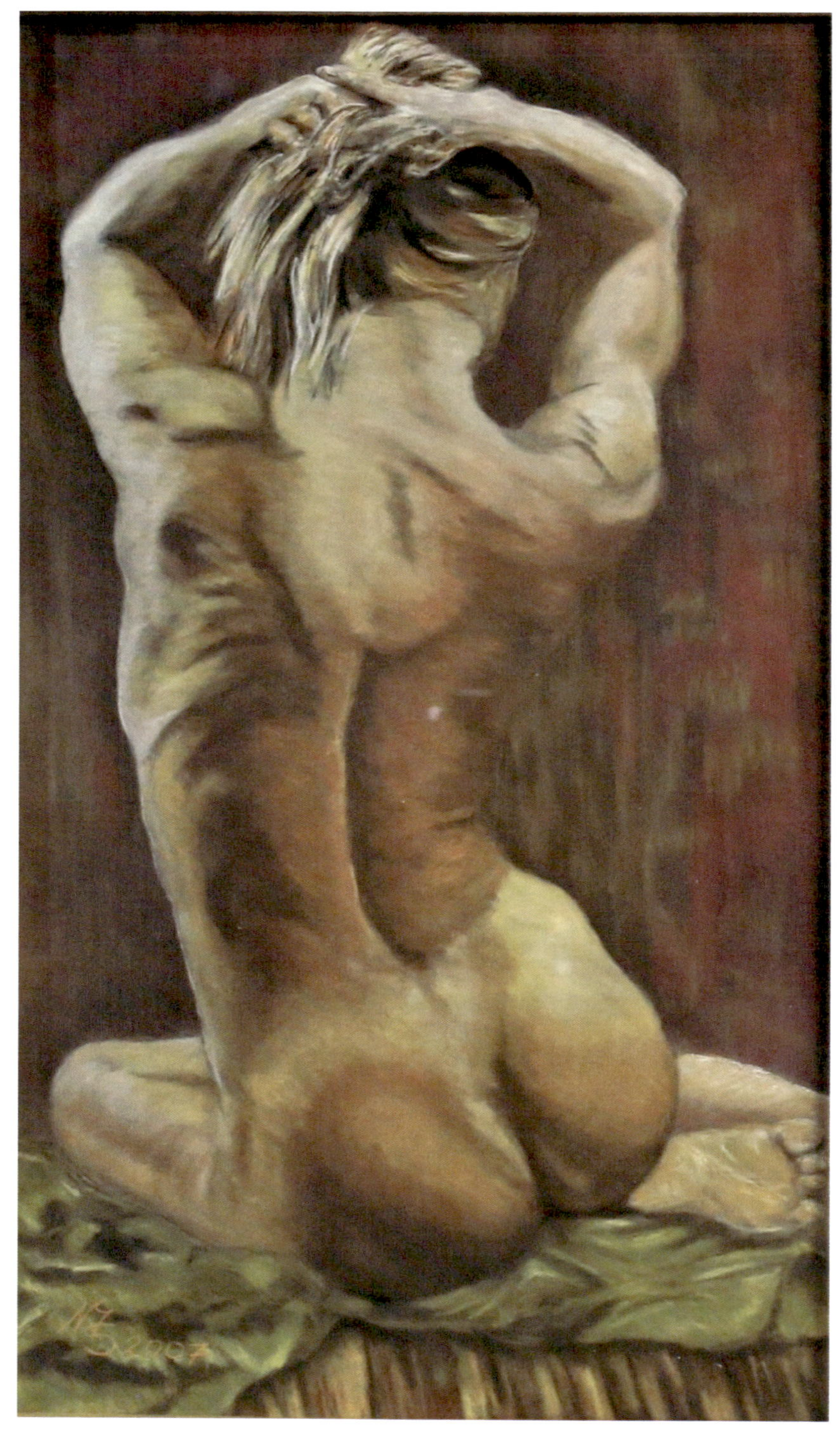

"Female Nude Sitting" Pastel on pastel board, 2007

Assignment: BK 5-03 Portraiture

Select a portrait subject. It can be a friend or relative, a pet, or yourself.

I recommend that you use a sheet of Canson Mi-Teintes drawing paper about 12" X 16". Choose a paper color close to the background color that you would like to use. Choose either a black charcoal pencil or white pastel pencil to draw the outline of your subject.

Before adding color, separate the dark tones and the light tones on the subject, using your paper color as the middle tone.

Add colors - note, hair will look more natural if you let some of the background colors show through and if your strokes follow in the direction of the hair.

When you are finished, lightly spray your work outside or in a well ventilated area with workable fixative.

Steps for Creating Animals

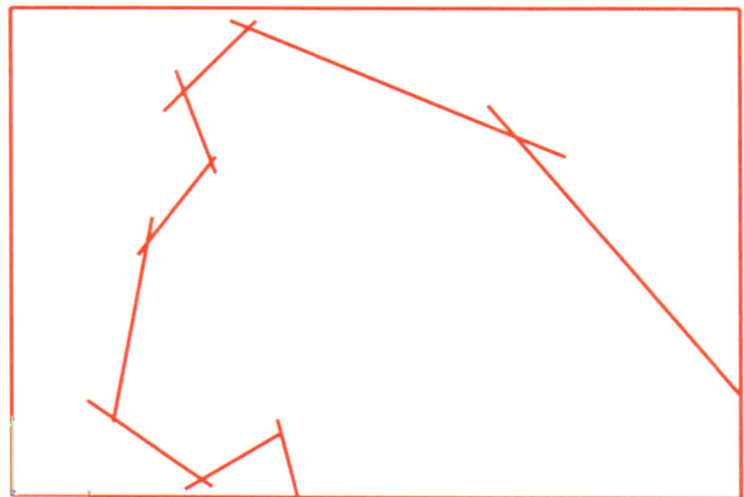

Step 1: Sketch Outline Envelope of main Subject.

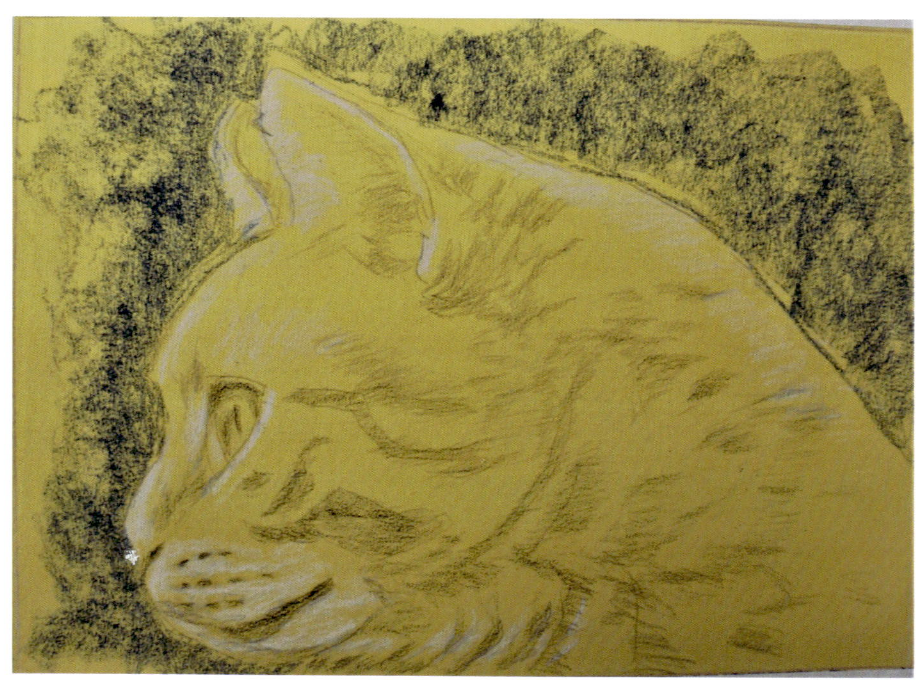

Step 2: Separate the light and dark shapes.

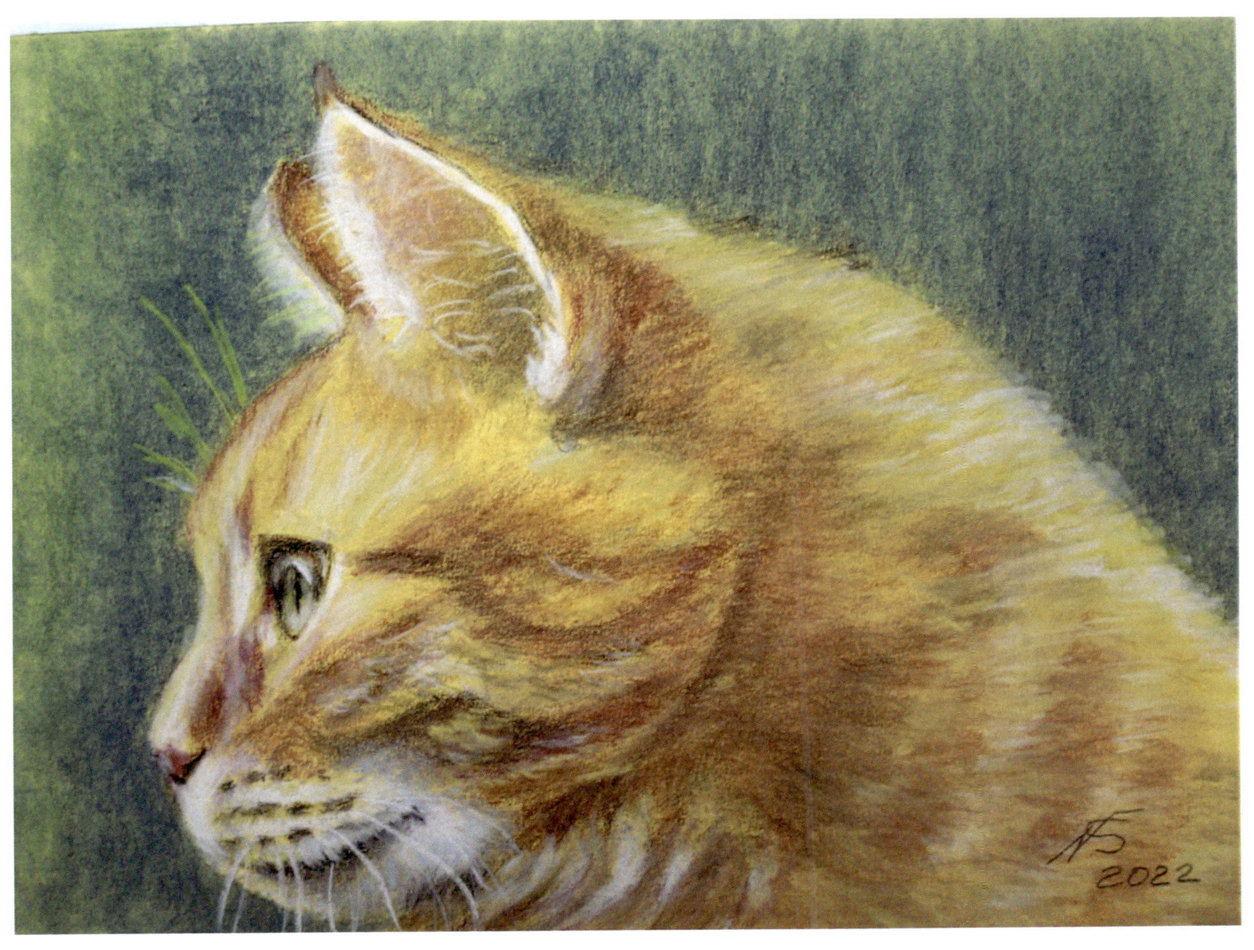

"Goldie Locks" Pastel on pastel Canson toned paper, 2022

Step 3: Add Color.

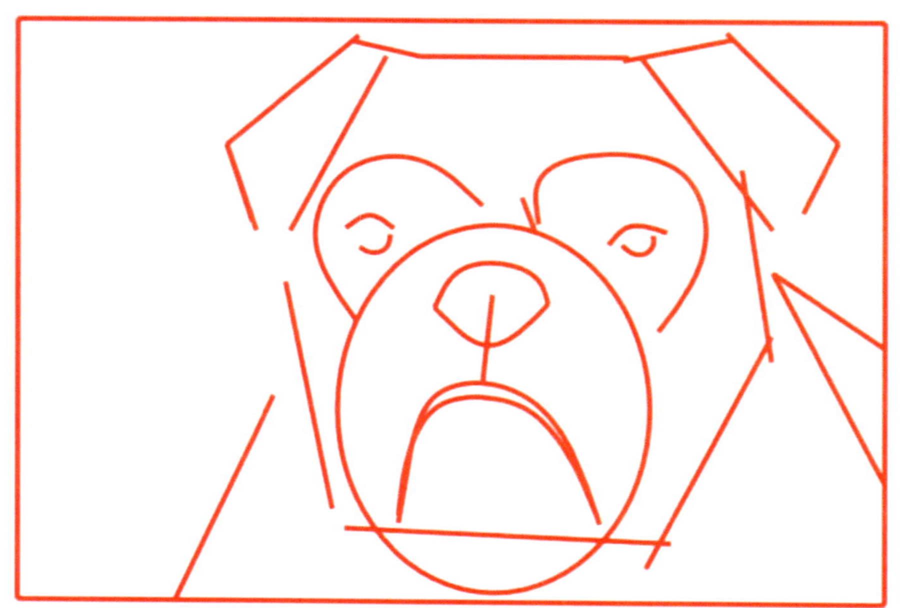

Step 1: Sketch Outline Envelope of main Subject.

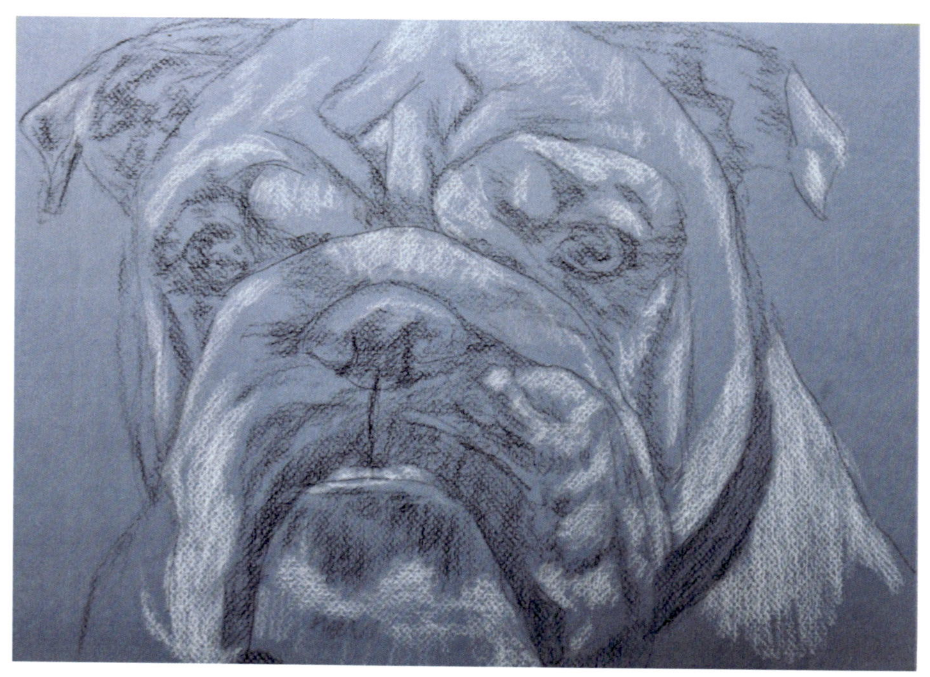

Step 2: Separate the light and dark shapes.

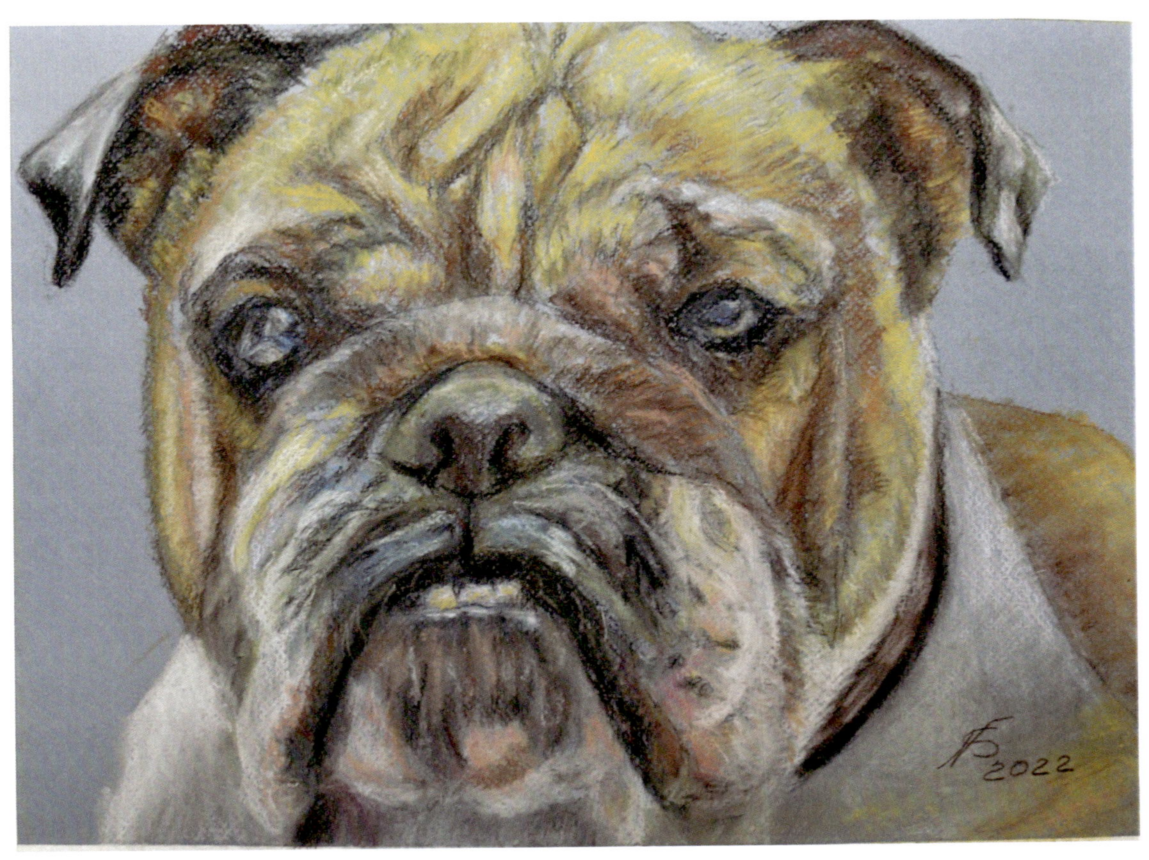

"Bruno" Pastel on pastel Canson toned paper, 2022

Step 3: Add Color.

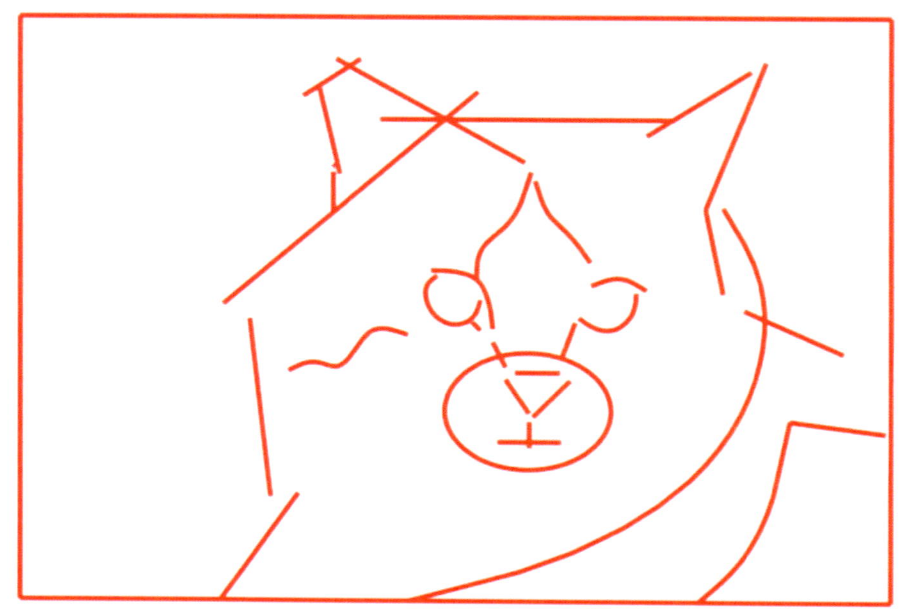

Step 1: Sketch Outline Envelope of main Subject.

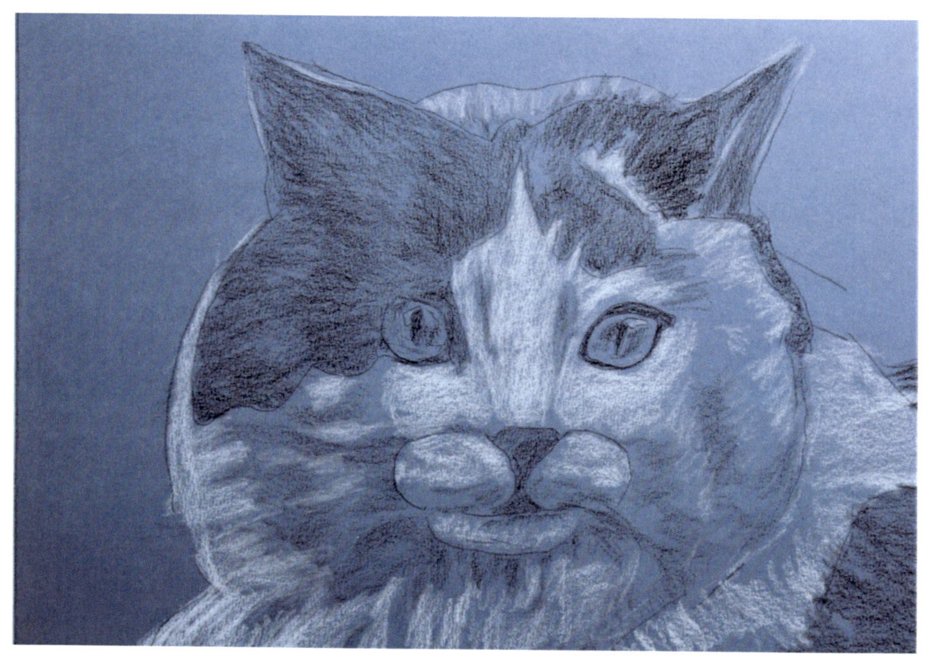

Step 2: Separate the light and dark shapes.

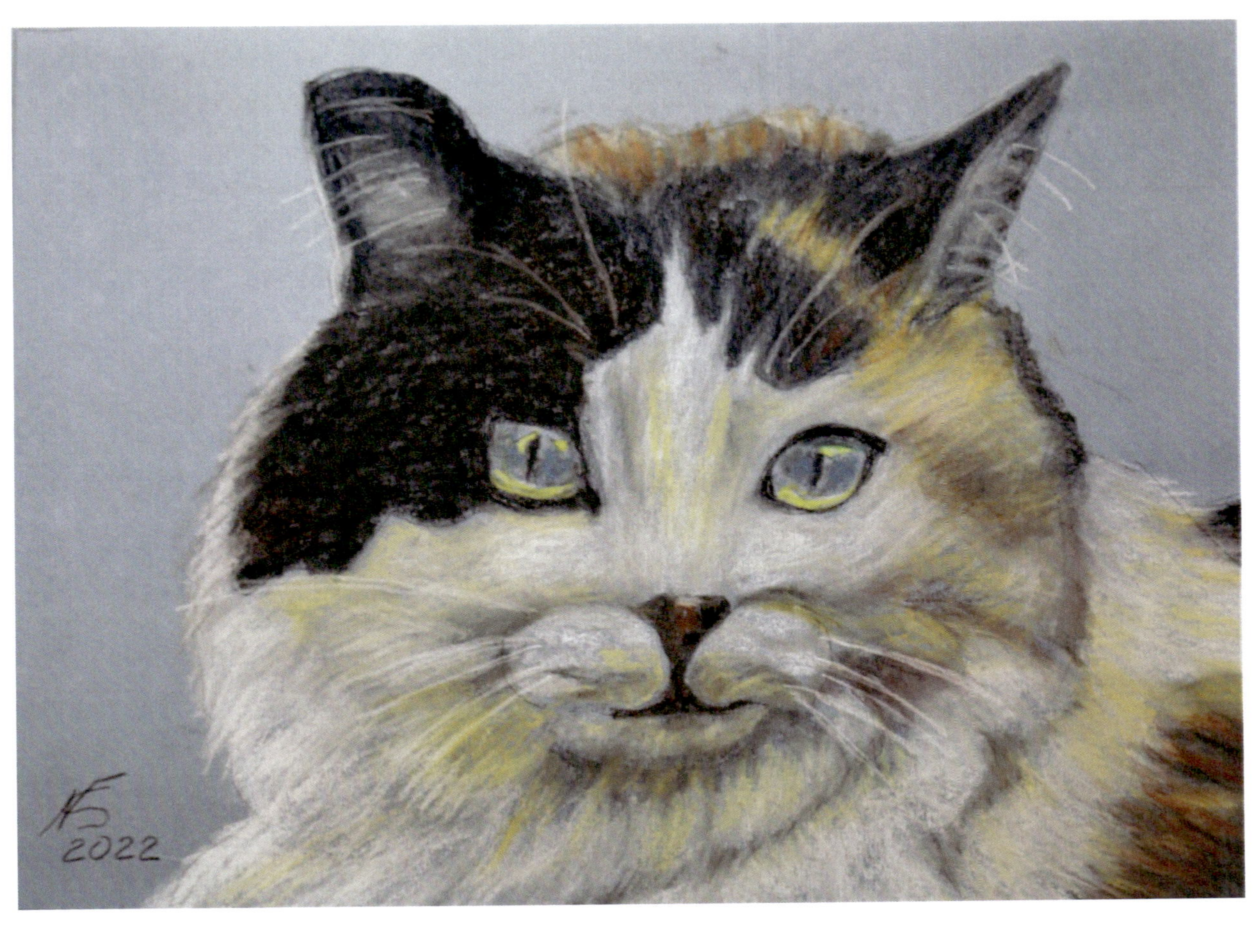

"Penny" Pastel on pastel Canson toned paper, 2022

Step 3: Add Color.

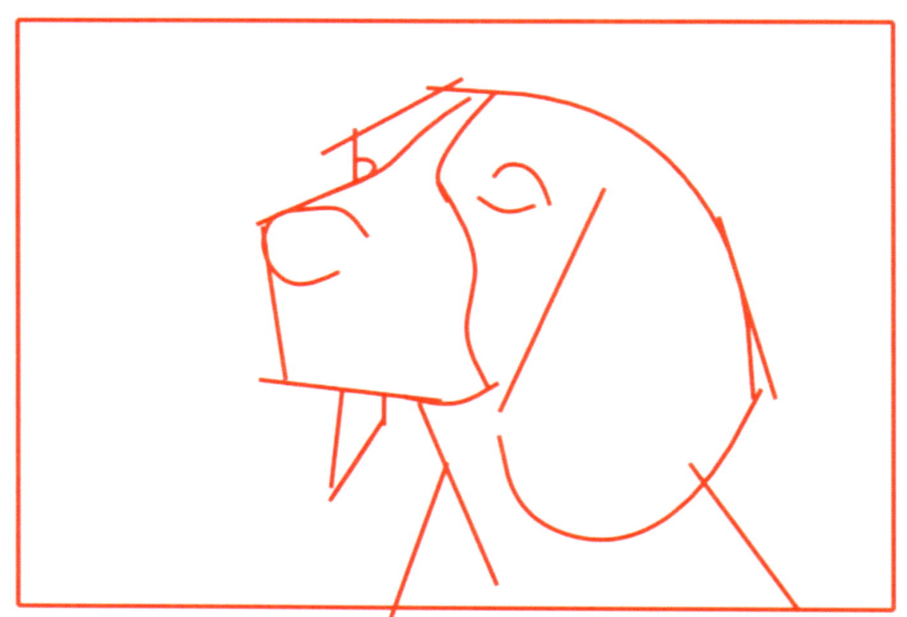

Step 1: Sketch Outline Envelope of main Subject.

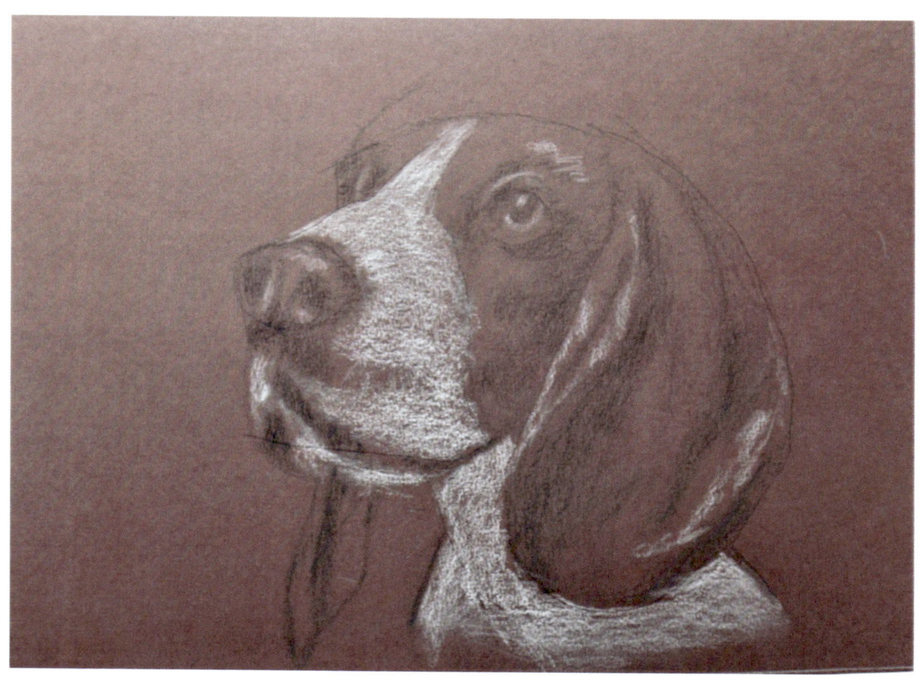

Step 2: Separate the light and dark shapes.

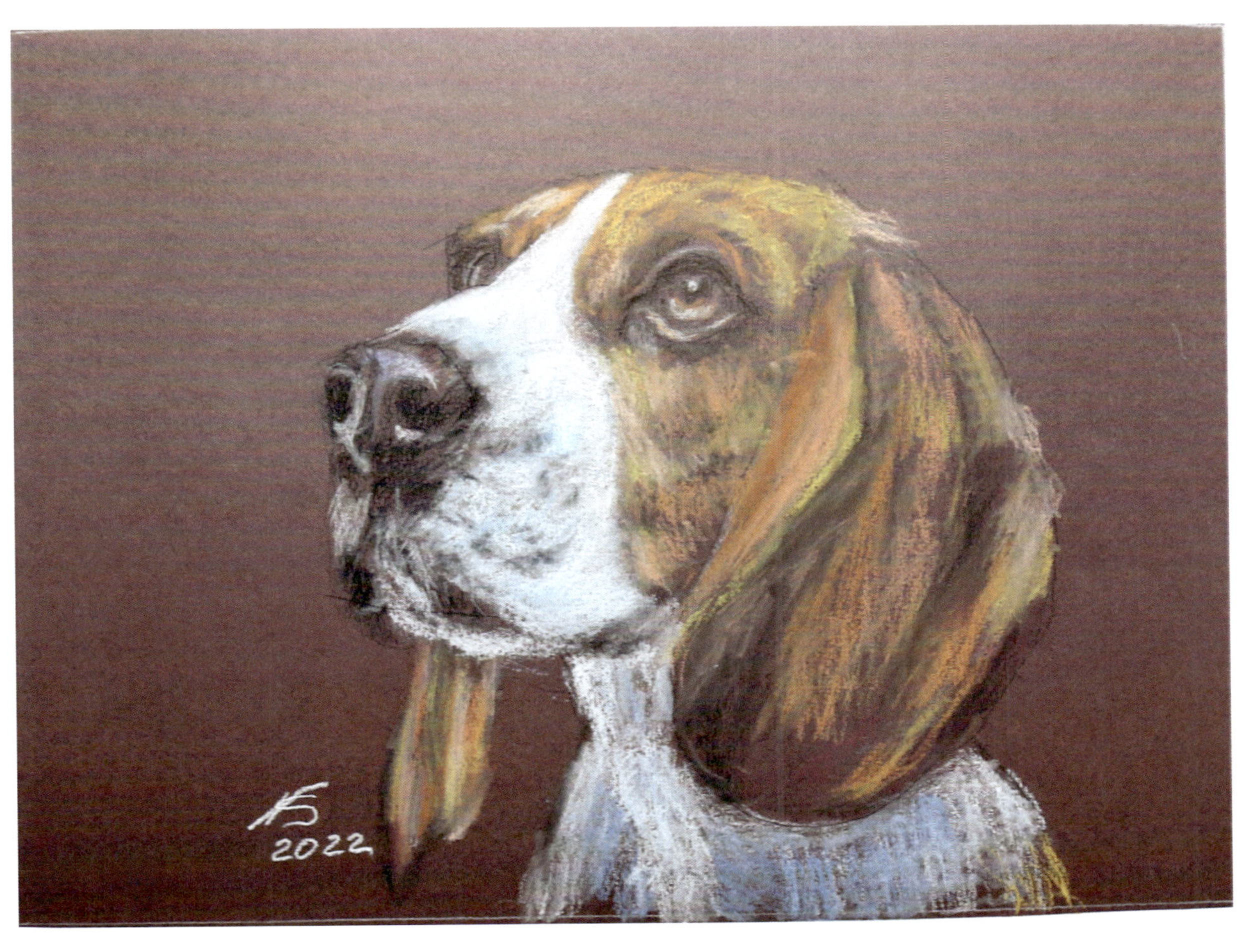

"Copper" Pastel on pastel Canson toned paper, 2022

Step 3: Add Color.

Introduction to Pastels Summary

In summarizing the "Introduction to Drawing" book five, we have experimented with art using pastels. This book involves advanced material because it includes so many aspects of art. We have explored various drawing methods and techniques in earlier books. With pastels, you are able to draw various lines and create wonderful drawings. Pastels offer an array of pastels colors, shades, and tints (soft, hard, pan, pencils) types and tools that make pastels interesting as a drawing, as well as a painting, method for creative artists.

Pastels offer artists an assortment of rich vibrant colors that can be experimented with in creating beautiful and expressive artworks. Unlike working with other painting mediums, pastels do not have a long drying time, letting artists quickly express themselves since they are free to spend countless hours in enjoying the pleasures of experimenting in the process of creating fine art paintings. I encourage artists to experiment with pastels using various surfaces (watercolor paper, pastel paper, also called ingres paper, Canson Mi-Teintes Drawing Paper, board, or canvas, etc.). I also find it helpful to use colored toned surfaces to work on when creating pastels artworks.

In this book, we learned about how to compose (arrange) still life subjects so that the artwork appears to be balanced and the main focal point or subject gets the highest attention of the viewers who should respond and interact visually with the artwork. We also worked with portraitures, as well as landscapes.

Pastels will increase both your drawing and painting skills as an artist. Pastels is perhaps the fastest way to refine your drawing skills so that you become a skilled painter, and are able to create artworks that are full of energy and emotion within the artworks.

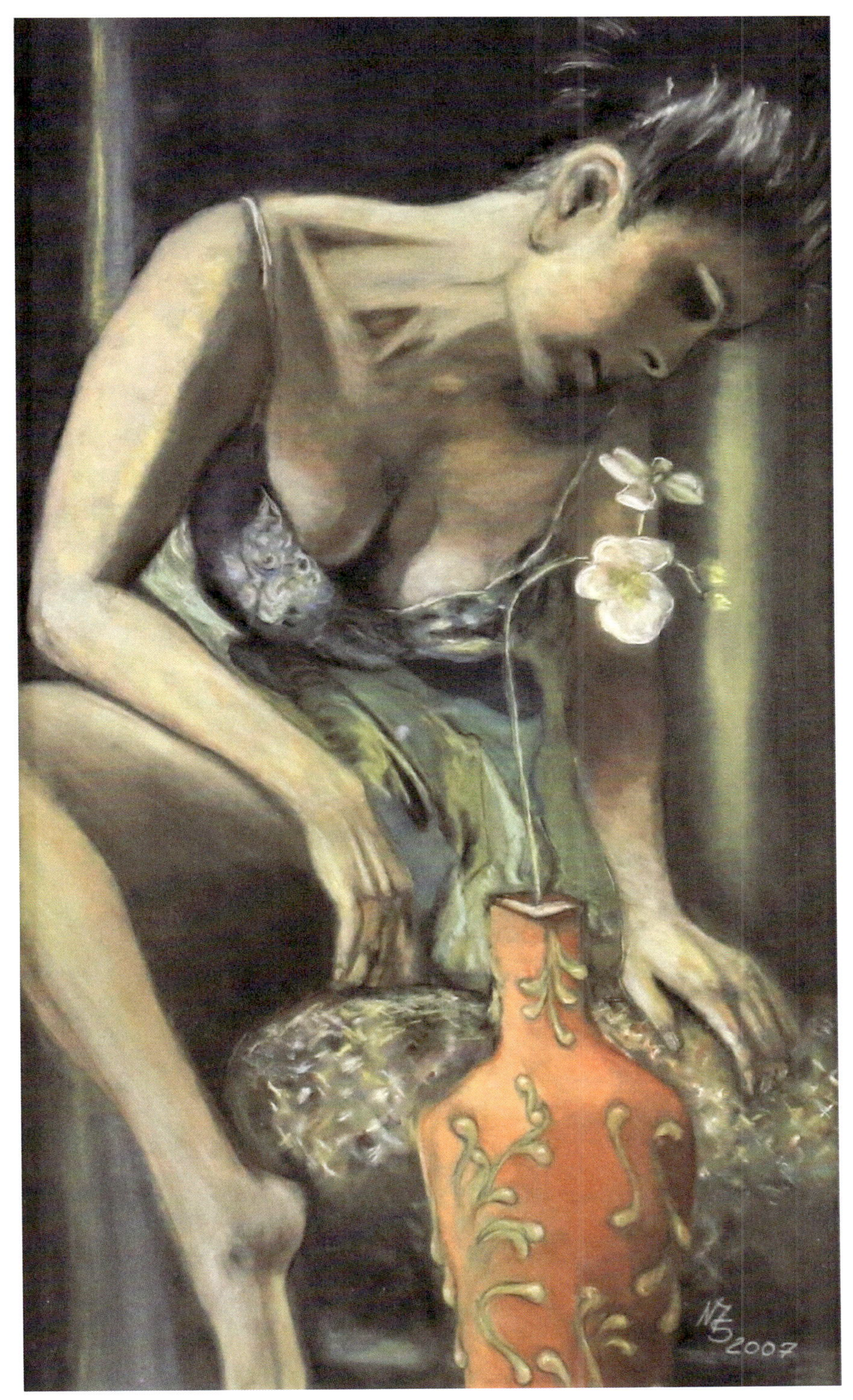

"Blossom" Pastel on pastel board, 2007

www.ingramcontent.com/pod-product-compliance
Lightning Source LLC
LaVergne TN
LVRC090254110826
845147LV00008B/735

* 9 7 8 1 9 5 5 1 0 4 1 3 5 *